Blackwork

Blackwork

Mary Gostelow

DOVER PUBLICATIONS, INC.
Mineola, New York

Published in Canada by General Publishing Company, Ltd., 30 Lesmill Road, Don Mills, Toronto, Ontario.

Bibliographical Note

This Dover edition, first published in 1998, is a slightly altered republication of the edition first published by B. T. Batsford Ltd., London, in 1976 and Van Nostrand Reinhold Company, New York, in 1977. Minor corrections have been made, and the sections "Organizations" and "Suppliers" have been omitted.

Library of Congress Cataloging-in-Publication Data

Gostelow, Mary.
    Blackwork / Mary Gostelow.
        p.   cm.
    Originally published: New York : Van Nostrand Reinhold, 1976.
    Includes bibliographical references and index.
    ISBN 0-486-40178-2 (pbk.)
    1. Blackwork embroidery.   I. Title.
TT778.B5G67   1998
746.44—dc21
                                          98–16111
                                            CIP

Manufactured in the United States of America
Dover Publications, Inc., 31 East 2nd Street, Mineola, N.Y. 11501

Contents

Acknowledgments

Blackwork has an undeniable mystique. Whilst studying this black-on-white embroidery I have become enthralled by its history. And I am fascinated by the amount of blackwork being done today in many different countries.

I could not have written this book without the encouragement and help of my photographer, my husband Martin Gostelow.

I have been continually helped, too, by many embroiderers and other specialists. For their assistance, therefore, in different ways, I should like especially to thank the following:

Dorothea Alonge; *Aramco World Magazine*, Mr Paul Hoye and Mr Bill Tracy; *Arnhem, Rijksmuseum voor Volkskunde* and Mevr A. Meulenbelt-Nieuwburg; Margaret Austin; Mrs C. B. Ayers; Miss Peggy Ballard; J. M. Bell; *Berlin, Staatliche Museen Preussischer Kulturbesitz Kunstgewerbemuseum* and Dr B. Mundt; Virginia Hill Bornemann; Agnes Bryson; Valerie Carson; Mrs Harvey Clinch; Mr J. M. Cobban; Alwynne Crowsen; *Dearborn, Greenfield Village and the Henry Ford Museum* and Mr Robert G. Wheeler; *Department of National Education of the Republic of South Africa*, Dr V. K. du Plessis, Miss Ida Blignaut and Mrs Anna Martin; *The Embroiderers' Guild*, Mr Joseph Gardner, Miss Joanna Hase and Mrs Avis Thompson; *The Embroiderers' Guild of America Inc.* and Mrs George Pilling IV; Mrs Joan Forsyth; *Glasgow Museums and Art Galleries,* Mr Brian Blench and Mr Wells; Constance Gully; Stella Hales; *The Hampton Institute*; Helen M. Healy; David Heathcote; *Heimilisidnadarfelags Islands* and Gerdur Hjorleifsdottir; *Hengrave Hall Centre* and Sister Mary Eucharia; Mr Colin Hoare; Natalie Howard; Mr and Mrs E. J. Ivory; Robin Jeffcoat; Sarah Johnstone; Mrs L. M. Jones; Heather Joynes; Karyn H. Katz; Marsha Katzman; Mrs Richard J. Lang; *Liberty and Co. Ltd* and Kathy Phillips; Mrs Bertram K. Little; Barbara Loftus; *The National Portrait Gallery* and The Education Department; *London, The Tate Gallery* and M. E. Fraser; *The Victoria and Albert Museum,*

Dr Roy Strong, Mr Donald King and Miss S. A. Levey; *The Lord Chamberlain's Office*, Miss Jane Hoos and Miss Sarah Wilson; Mrs Murray Lowry; *City of Manchester Art Galleries*, Mr Julian Treuherz; Cynthia Marks; Mrs H. J. Maxwell; Moyra McNeill; The Earl of Moray; Sir Owen Morshead GCVO; Mr J. L. Nevinson; *New York, Metropolitan Museum of Art*. Miss Jean Mailey and Barbara Teague; Mrs Daphne Nicholson; *Nottingham, Castlegate Museum of Costume and Textiles* and Mr Jeremy W. Farrell; Norma Papish; George Philip & Son Ltd; Barbara Price; Sir John and Lady Carew Pole; *The Public Record Office* and M. M. Condon; Mr Sohel Fuad Rached; Mrs Reichenbach; Mrs Gillian Ridler; Mrs E. de la Rosa; Margaret Ross; Mrs Cynthia Russell; Wendy Saunders; Cynthia Sparks; *Stellenbosch University* and Mrs Pieter Knye; Mrs Ezanne Steward; Nancy Stolarsky; *Stonyhurst College* and the Warden's Secretary: *Toronto, The Royal Ontario Museum*, Mrs K. B. Brett and Mr John E. Vollmer; Betty Vanderbilt; Mrs J. Nel Warden; Mrs Richard Van Wagenen; Mrs Hetsie van Wyk; Maxine Ziemba and Jane D. Zimmerman.

Mary Gostelow
Milton Abbas 1976

1 The History of Blackwork

Blackwork, black-on-white embroidery, has sometimes been called 'Spanish work'. And the conception of blackwork is often erroneously attributed to that celebrated sixteenth-century Spanish lady, Catherine of Aragon.

Poor Catherine! She was born in 1485 in Alcala de Henares, Spain. Her parents' marriage was a political arrangement, intended to unite the two great Iberian houses of Aragon, in eastern Spain, and Castile, to the west. Ferdinand II and his queen, Isabella, were sometimes known as the 'Reyes Católicos' (the 'Catholic Kings') and they are today remembered for many of their innovations like the Council of the Inquisition (1483). Their children were all destined for unfortunate lives: Joanna ('La Loca') was to go mad after the death of her husband, Philip I ('The Handsome'), ruler of the Burgundian Netherlands, their only son died at the age of nineteen—and there was Catherine. . . .

Catherine was sent to England in 1501 to marry Prince Arthur, eldest son of King Henry VII. The Prince died the following year and shortly afterwards his young widow was betrothed to his brother, Prince Henry. They finally married when Henry ascended to the throne, as Henry VIII, in 1504. By 1518 Queen Catherine had given birth to six children, all of whom, except her daughter Mary (later Queen Mary), were either stillborn or died in infancy.

It is ironic to note that one of Catherine's emblems was said to have been the pomegranate, a pagan symbol of fertility and regeneration. But, alas, the fiery Henry was desperate for a male heir and he wanted to be rid of this queen. Legal and papal intervention were invoked to annul the marriage. Although Pope Clement VII declared the marriage valid, Henry nonetheless preferred the annulment offered by Thomas Cranmer, Archbishop of Canterbury. He thus went his own way, and to his next queen. Catherine, shunned by royal decree, spent her last years in semi-isolation. She died in Kimbolton in 1536.

1 Catherine of Aragon, artist unknown, 56.5 cm × 43.8 cm (22¼ in × 17¼ in). *(National Portrait Gallery)*

The National Portrait Gallery, London, has a portrait (figure 1) showing the queen standing in front of two columns, their capitals decorated with acanthus leaves. The artist, who did not sign his work, has painted a contemplative and rather solid, unimaginative figure. Catherine is wearing a typical Tudor cap with side lappets pinned up. The square neck band of her chemise is decorated with what looks like scrolled blackwork.

Catherine is certainly known to have had items of black-on-white decoration in her first trousseau. In her important treatise *Needlework as Art*, Lady Marian Alford wrote that the queen

'introduced the Spanish taste in embroidery, which was then white or black silk and gold "lace stitches" on fine linen. This went by the name of "Spanish work" and continued to be the fashion down to and through the reign of Mary Tudor, who remained faithful to the traditions of her mother's and her grandmother's work. Catherine of Aragon learned her craft from her mother, Queen Isabella, who always made her husband's shirts'. (Lady Marian Alford, *Needlework as Art*, Sampson Low, 1886, p. 383.)

Lady Alford, for all her admirable work in promulgating the art of embroidery generally, must nevertheless not be taken as infallible.

It was common knowledge that Catherine was a needlewoman. Both she and King Henry loved beautiful things. A contemporary English writer, Edward Hall (died 1547) included in his *Holinshed's Chronicles of England, Scotland and Ireland* (published posthumously in 1580) the following account of the coronation, on 21 June 1509:

'If I should declare, what pain, labour and diligence, the Taylers, Embroiderours, and Golde Smithes took, both to make and devise garmentes, for Lordes, Ladies, Knightes and Esquires and also for deckying, trappying and adornyng of Coursers, Ianets and Palffreis it wer to long to rehersse.'

The King himself was dressed in 'a jacket and cote of raised gold, the Placard embrowdered with Diamonds, Rubies, Emeraudes, greate Pearles and other riche stones'.

The splendid array of colour thus portrayed was undoubtedly the work of professional embroiderers (it is known that one leading needleman, a certain Anthony was paid 4d a day for his labours at that time). But Catherine and her ladies could possibly have embroidered costume and other items for less extravagant occasions. A century after her death, John Taylor wrote *The Needle's*

Excellency, described as 'a New Booke wherein are divers Admirable Workes wrought with the Needle, Newly invented and cut in Copper for the pleafure and profit of the Induftrious' and printed for one Iames Boler, 'To be Sold at the Signe of the Marigold in Paules Churchyard, 1636'. In this fascinating little book, Taylor wrote:

'I Read that in the feventh King Henries Raigne
Faire Katharine, Daughter to the Castile King,
Came into England with a pompous traine
of Spanifh Ladies, which fhe thence did bring.
She to the eight King Henry married was
And afterwards divorc'd, where vertuenfly
(Although a Queene) yet fhe her dayes did paffe,
In working the Needle curioufly,
As in the Towre, and place more befide,
Her excellent memorials may be feene:
Whereby the Needles prayfe is dignifide
By her fair Ladies, and herfeilfe, a Queene,
Thus for her paines, here her reward is just,
Her workes proclaime her prayfe, though fhe be duft.'

We know, therefore, that Catherine did undoubtedly do some kind of needlework. But did she do any *blackwork*? The association of the queen with this kind of embroidery has been stressed by leading embroidery historians like Ellen Masters. In her book *The Gentlewoman's Book of Art Needlework*, she stated that 'several specimens of the embroidery executed by this queen are still known as "Spanish work". (Ellen Masters, *The Gentlewoman's Book of Art Needlework*, Henry, 1893, p. 41.)

The term 'Spanish work' was in general usage until circa 1530. A 1523 inventory of Agnes Hungerford's belongings mentions 'viij partletts of sypers iij of them garnyshed with golde and the rest with Spanyshe warke'. (Public Record Office, State Papers Domestic, Henry VIII, SP1/27, f. 93.) By 1530 the term 'blackwork' was used for costume decorated with black-on-white embroidery, a fashion that was to be particularly important until about 1560. The one blackwork illustration in Henny Harald Hansen's *Costume Cavalcade* (Methuen, 1956, p. 313), for example, is dated circa 1540 and is of a gentleman wearing a shirt with blackwork decoration.

It is often erroneously assumed that when Catherine brought with her, in her 1501 trousseau, pieces of 'Spanish work' decoration, she was introducing it to English taste. In point of fact, however, this form of stitching was known in England long before. Chaucer makes mention of it in his *Canterbury Tales*, written during the last decade of his life (that is to say, during the period 1390–1400). The poet had himself become a widower recently and his talent as raconteur is particularly poignant in 'The Mylleres Tale':

'Fair was the yonge wyf, and therwithal
As eny wesil hir body gent and smal.
A seynt sche werede, barrad al of silk;
A barm-cloth eek as white as morne mylk
Upon hir lendes, ful of many a gore.
Whit was hir smok and browdid al byfore
And eek bygyade on hir coler aboute
Of cole-blak silk, withinne and eeke withoute.'
(*Chaucer's Canterbury Tales for the Modern Reader*, ed. Arthur Burrell, Everyman's Library, Dent, 1908, p. 77.)

The operative lines, being interpreted, read: 'Her smock was white and embroidered in front and behind with coal-black silk and embroidered also on the inside and outside of the collar.'

How common 'cole-blak silk' embroidery was in England and western Europe in the late fourteenth century is not definitely recorded. It is possible to conjecture that Catherine had, in Spain, developed a penchant for this form of embroidered decoration and thus could have asked to have some pieces of blackwork included in her trousseau when she came to marry her first husband. She could thus have set a fashion in the way that royal marriages or similar national events still today often act as precursors for current taste: although Berlin wool work embroidery was already known and practised throughout Europe long before Queen Victoria married her cousin Prince Albert of Saxe–Coburg–Gotha in 1840, the Germanic strength of wool work panels became more noticeable in England thereafter and, in our own century and in another decorative art form, Princess Anne must surely have prolonged the life of the 'Gucci-bit' shoes and belts first worn by international jet-setters but soon available generally from many well-known department stores. In this way, therefore, Catherine may have put her seal of approval on a certain element of Spanish taste and design.

To trace the heritage of early sixteenth-century 'Spanish taste' it is necessary briefly to look at the history of the Iberian peninsula. Looking at a map of Europe (figure 2) at that time, the power of the Spanish rulers is immediately apparent.

From A.D. 711 on, the southern part of Spain was settled by Arabs from northern Africa. They brought with them an Islamic artistic expression which was assimilated throughout much of Spain.

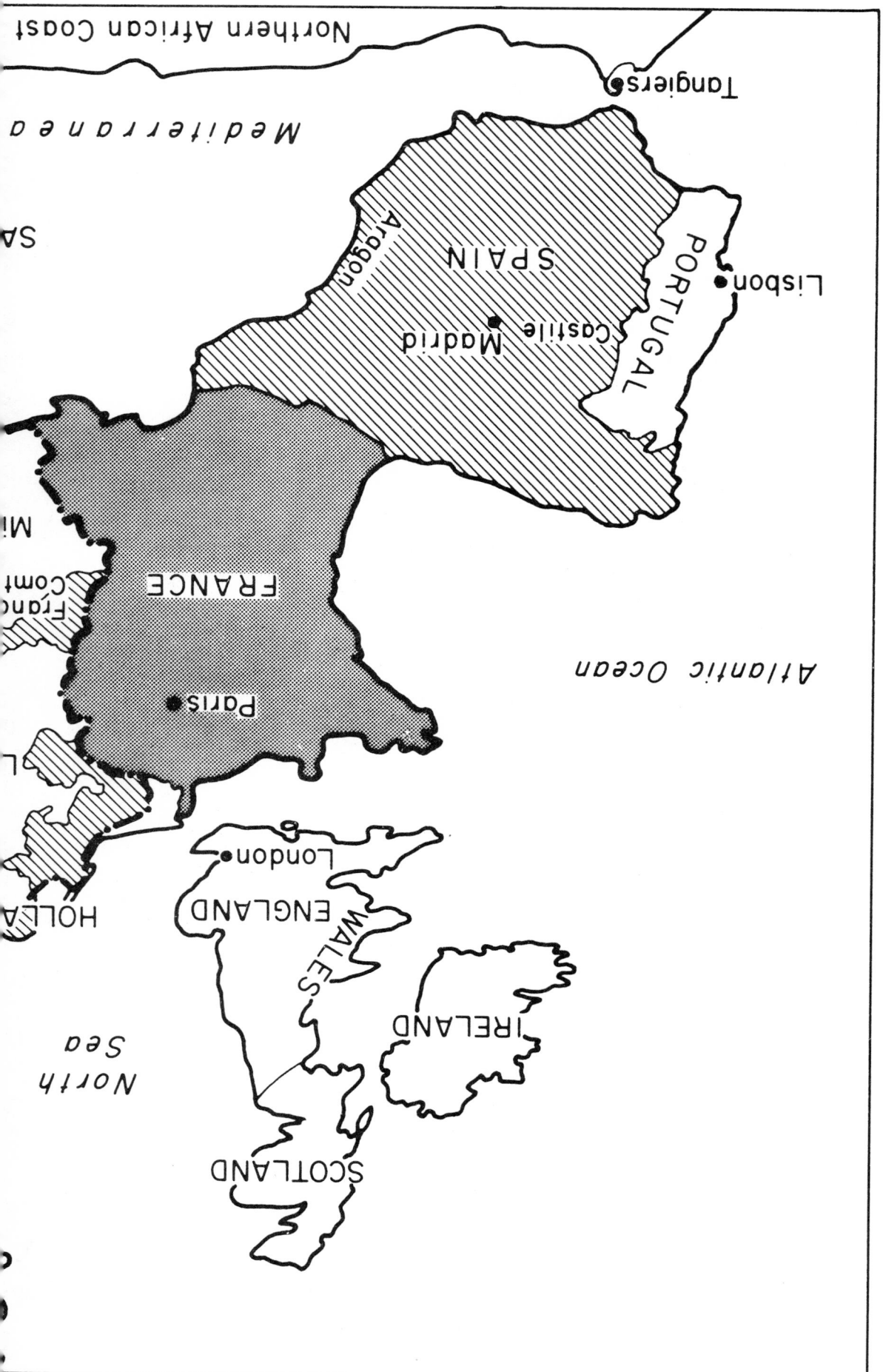

Northern African Coast

Mediterranea

SA

Tangiers

Aragon

SPAIN

PORTUGAL

Castile Madrid

Lisbon

Mi

FRANCE

Franc
Com

Atlantic Ocean

Paris

HOLLA

London

ENGLAND

WALES

IRELAND

North
Sea

SCOTLAND

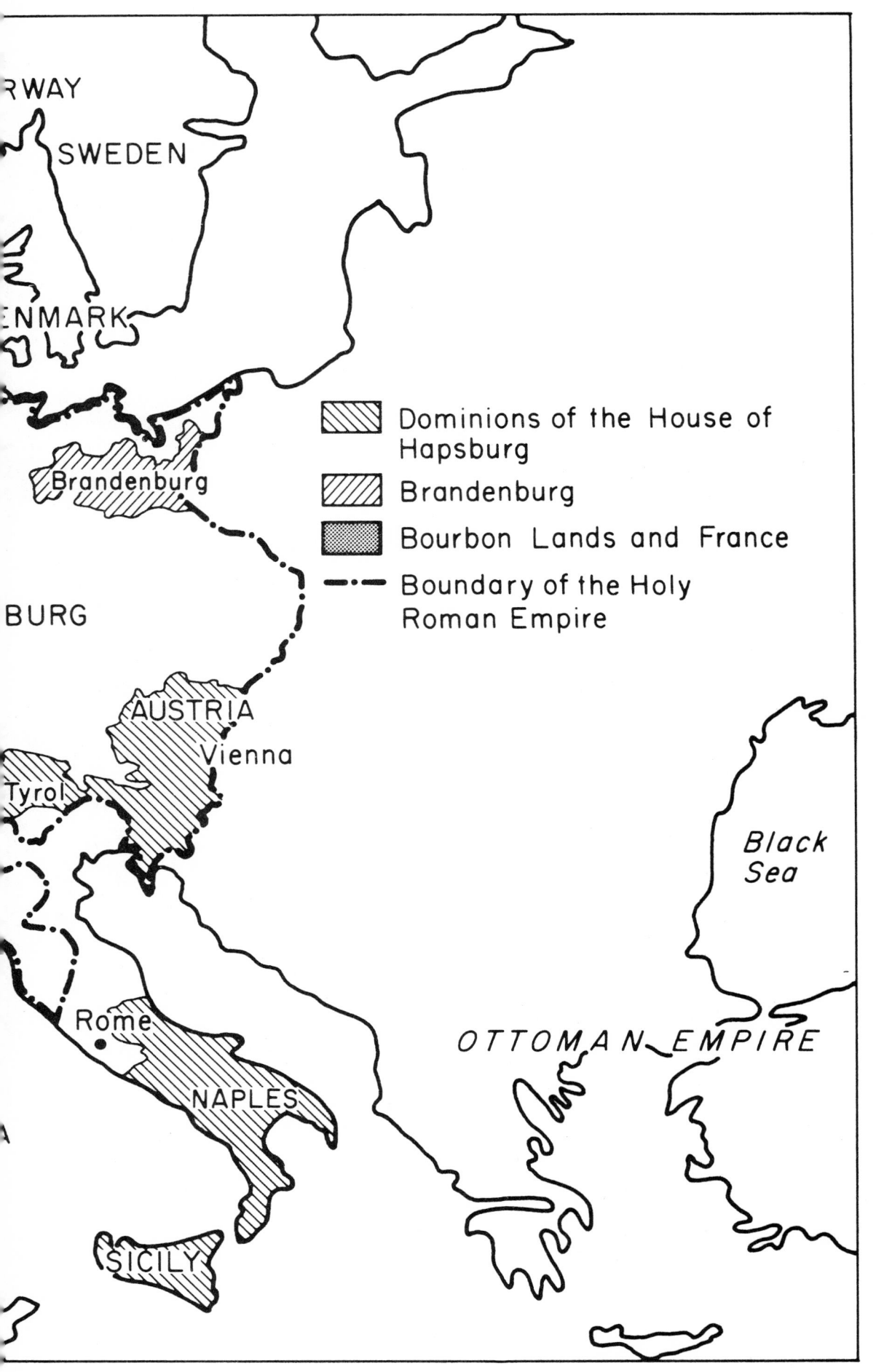

Dominions of the House of Hapsburg

Brandenburg

Bourbon Lands and France

Boundary of the Holy Roman Empire

Overleaf:
2 Map of Europe at the beginning of the sixteenth century. *(Map reproduced by kind permission of George Philip and Son Ltd, publishers of* Muir's Historical Atlas*)*

Spanish noblemen were keen to be associated with many forms of art. Both Ferdinand and Isabella were keen patrons and the latter, in particular, had a fine collection of paintings, many of them possibly by her own personal court painter, the Fleming Juan de Flandes. Isabella, like her daughter, has gone down in the eternal annals of the arts: the multi-faceted architectural decoration invariably associated with Spain and usually called 'plateresque' is sometimes known as 'Isabelline' in her honour.

It is easy to visualize how many of the fluted, scrolled and carefully controlled geometric patterns associated with Moorish tiles, doorways and design in general could have passed to Spanish thought. And, from there, the same arabesques and scrolls could have passed with Catherine when she came to England.

This, then, is a theory not for the *introduction* of blackwork but, rather, for the increased popularity of what was already known. The Moorish style, known variously as 'Moresque' or 'arabesque', is typified by exactly proportioned floral fluting and interlacing. This kind of pattern again has debatable ancestry, for it is found in Hellenistic art, principally from Asia Minor, from early times: the British Museum has a delicate silver cup with repoussé decoration of arabesque-shaped design, 1st century A.D. But in the Moslem world the patterns became particularly popular around 1100. Arabesque design transposed easily to black-on-white embroidery. Was it, therefore, from Moorish design in general that blackwork embroidery evolved?

An alternative school of thought suggests that blackwork in England in the early sixteenth century developed from the linear embroideries that had long been worked in Holbein (double-running) stitch in Europe. This theory is put forward by Patricia Wardle in *Guide to English Embroidery* (HMSO, 1970). In her coverage of blackwork she further suggests that part of the reason for the popularity of this form of stitching in England was the ease with which it lent itself to stitched versions of contemporary linear pen illustrations.

If this theory of European heritage is correct, the case for a twelfth-century embroidery being 'the oldest known piece of blackwork' has some validity. Alas, the evidence for this supposition is no longer even fragmentary. The embroidery thought to have been one of the first examples of monochrome (or one-colour thread) embroidery was destroyed when its last home, the Schlossmuseum in Berlin, was razed during the Second World War.

3 Altar fragment from Fulda. 1170—80. The
panel, 113 cm × 116 cm (44½ in × 45½ in),
was in the Schlossmuseum in Berlin, razed
during the Second World War

The piece consisted of a fragment of an altar panel (figure 3), thought to have come from the Rhineland, possibly from Fulda in West Germany. Four of the scenes on the panel showed biblical events. In one pair of vignettes, the Annunciation is followed by the Visitation. In the other pair, the Nativity is matched with the Adoration of the Magi, with the names of the three kings illuminated in so personal a way that the embroiderer, working the letters 'MELCHIOR' from top to bottom, left no room for the 'o' and 'R' and had accordingly to turn a sharp right-angled corner. Both pairs of tableaux are surrounded by reversing fleur-de-lis scrolls, worked in outline, with exotic birds to each corner of the surround.

Inscriptions above the embroidered pictures are in mediaeval Latin. The top line of lettering reads: 'Concipit hē (hunc) virgo quē (quem) vates . . . ī (in) alvo' ('The Virgin conceives Him when the prophet (foretold?) in her womb'). The lower line of lettering reads: 'Ecce novi regis micā (micat) in dex (dextra?) stella sabaeis' ('Behold the star of the new King shines (in the east?) for the Sabaeans (Arabians)'). This extraordinary embroidery was dated by Schuette and Müller-Christensen (*The Art of Embroidery*, Thames and Hudson, 1964) as circa 1170–80. Mr Donald King, of the Victoria and Albert Museum, confirms this possible date although he admits that the cloth might have been worked a few years later.

At first glance a twelfth-century identification—over a hundred years before the debut of the Syon cope and other famous early *Opus Anglicanum* ('English work') embroideries—seems inordinately premature. But it must be remembered that, although in Britain after the Conquest of 1066, with a delightful folk attitude showing in embroideries like the Bayeux 'tapestry' (worked around 1070 and now to be seen in the Musée de la Reine Mathilde in Bayeux, Calvados), counterparts being produced elsewhere in the world were already incredibly sophisticated. The 'Coronation mantle', worked in the royal workshops of Palermo for the coronation of the Norman king Roger II in 1133–4, is remarkably complex in its design and craftsmanship. Now housed in the Kunsthistorisches Museum in Vienna, the mantle is 3.4 m (11 ft 2 in) across and has gorgeous pairs of camels and lions flanking a tree of life, the whole worked in silks, metal threads and pearls on a ground of red silk. The advanced make-up of the Palermo embroidery shows it to be quite possible that the Fulda work could indeed have been produced some forty years later.

Age apart, however, the Fulda fragment is—or was—outstanding. It was embroidered in chain stitch, in linen and silk on a ground of fine linen. The only tragedy is that the blackwork student must today suffice with studying the embroidery through the writings of others, notably through Otto von Falke's description in *Berliner Museums—Berichte aus den Preussischen Kunstsammlungen,* vol. XLII, 1921, p. 71.

2 English Blackwork

In 1601 'Bess of Hardwick' (1520–1608) was installed in the new house built on the site of her birthplace, Hardwick Hall in Derbyshire. The inventory of possessions at that time is laced with embroidery details. In the 'Newe building at Hardwick, the Turret Chamber' were

> 'three Curtins wrought with black silk nedlework uppon fine holland Cloth with buttons and lowpes of black silk on the sides. Partes to goe about the sides of the bed at the bottome of cloth of golde and Crimson velvet, fringed with black and yellowe silk frenge, a Curtin of darnix and a peece of buckerom about the bed to Cover it'. (*The Hardwick Hall Inventories of 1601*, ed. Lindsay Boynton, The Furniture History Society, London, 1971, p. 23.)

'Bess of Hardwick' is one of the outstanding embroiderers of all time. She must also go into the annals of *dames formidables* of any age and, before studying her blackwork, it is valuable as a preamble to look at the lady herself.

She survived four husbands. She was married first, when twelve years old, to Robert Barlow, a neighbouring landowner who died the following year, leaving his estate to his young widow. In 1547 she married Sir William Cavendish, Treasurer of the King's Chamber, by whom she had six children, her only offspring. Widowed once more, she married Sir William St Lowe, Captain of the Guard to Elizabeth I and Grand Butler of England, and her last husband was George Talbot, sixth Earl of Shrewsbury.

It was during this final marriage that Bess came into contact with the imprisoned Mary Queen of Scots, who was under the care of the Earl of Shrewsbury for fifteen years, from 1569 to 1584. Queen Mary, another famous embroiderer, was at one time thought to have worked some of the hangings now to be seen at Hardwick Hall (property of The National Trust), although there is no record of her ever having visited the site during her lifetime and the consensus today is that the Hardwick embroideries were mainly from Bess's needle. The two ladies differed in their embroidery styles. Bess was an ambitious personality in many respects and she preferred cosmopolitan themes like 'Europa and the Bull' and 'Mahomet prostrate before faith'. Queen Mary, less international in her embroidery design, showed an unmistakable sense of humour when working allegories of her feelings about her captor, her cousin Elizabeth, as exemplified in a cushion, one of the few Marian pieces to be seen at Hardwick.

Many fine sets of household furnishings were decorated with blackwork embroidery. In some cases those collections are today still in situ. In other instances the collections have been removed to the custody of museums.

The Victoria and Albert Museum, unique in its collection of all types of embroidery, has an outstanding array of blackwork furnishings. One of these is a cover (figure 4) worked in silks and silver–gilt threads on a long warp length of linen, the selvedge running along one side. It is embroidered in stem stitch, back stitch, chain stitch, plaited braid stitch and buttonhole stitch. The design shows flowers and fruits separated by scrolled foliage.

4 Detail of blackwork cover 2.69 m × 73.6 cm (8 ft 10 in × 29 in), worked in silks and silver–gilt threads on a long warp length of linen. The pattern is worked in stem stitch, back stitch, chain stitch, plaited braid stitch and buttonhole stitch. *(Victoria and Albert Museum, Crown Copyright, No. T.531–1897)*

5 Cushion cover, 88.9 cm × 49.5 cm (35 in × 19½ in), embroidered in back stitch, chain stitch, braid stitch, buttonhole stitch and with cording. *(Victoria and Albert Museum, Crown Copyright, No. T.82–1924)*

Another beautiful blackwork item in the same museum is a cushion cover (figure 5). It is embroidered in silks on linen, in back stitch, chain stitch, braid stitching, buttonhole stitch and with cording. At one time it was thought that this piece was the reverse of a similar blackwork embroidery (Victoria and Albert Museum, No. T.81 1924), but the two panels are probably complementary. No two-sided embroidered cushions are recorded but similar pairs of cushions were sometimes found, each with embroidery on one side only. One such pair of blackwork pillow covers was sold at Sotheby's on 1 April 1934 (Lot 173) as part of the collection of Sir William Lawrence.

Provenance of embroidery is always of interest. The Royal Ontario Museum, Toronto, has a pillow cover (figure 6) from the collection of Louisa, Marchioness of Waterford. The cover is embroidered in black silk floss and silver-gilt threads on a ground of white linen. The stitching is plaited braid stitch, chain stitch, interlaced four-legged knot stitch, detached buttonhole stitch, stem stitch, double-running (Holbein) stitch and there are silver–gilt 'spangles', formed by cross and double-cross stitches of silver–gilt thread worked into adjoining silk stitches. More silver–gilt thread has then been intertwined to form a 'basket' of discs.

6 Cover, late sixteenth century, embroidered in black silks and silver–gilt thread, 48 cm × 75 cm (18½ in × 29½ in). *(Royal Ontario Museum, Toronto, No. 923.4.73)*

This pillow cover (or 'bere') is dated late sixteenth century. It has been fully written up in the Royal Ontario Museum's book *English Embroidery in the Royal Ontario Museum* (Royal Ontario Museum, 1972), by the immediate past curator of the Textile Department, Mrs K. B. Brett. The lattice design of the cover has large rosettes at the intersections. The interstices are filled with alternate rows of birds and flowers. There is a crane (symbolizing vigilance), a turkey (symbolizing earth), a dove (symbolizing peace), a phoenix (symbolizing regeneration) and a carnation (often a betrothal symbol). An alternative theory, expounded by Mr Donald King, is that the non-floral representations stand for the four elements of earth, water, air and fire (ibid., p. 6).

Such exquisite covers and hangings were always worked on a ground of linen, a bast fibre culled from the flax *Linum usitatissimum*. The stalks of the plant were retted, dried, crushed and beaten to produce linen thread, valued for its strength and durability. Although it was difficult to dye linen to an even colouring, it bleached to a pure white which made it particularly suitable a ground fabric for the contrast effect of blackwork embroidery. The higher-quality linens tended to become even whiter, smoother and more lustrous with age.

The finest linens, used for blackwork costume accessories like ruffs, cuffs and sleeves, were later to include 'lawn', named after the French town of Laon. It is a very fine semi-transparent cloth also known as 'cloth of Rheims'. There was also 'cambric', a similar cloth first manufactured at the city of Cambrai. 'Holland' (or 'Hollands'), a plain-weave unbleached or dull-finished linen first imported from the Netherlands, but later from elsewhere in Europe, was used for shirt panels. Less expensive items were made from 'lockeram' (or 'lockram'), which was a coarser linen, 'harden', which was a linen made from tow, 'sammeron' and many other linens not usually individually identified today.

Imported fabrics were available from merchants and, later, from establishments run by such gentlemen as Mr Benjamin Cole, a draper who operated 'at the Sun in St Paul's Churchyard'. His tradesmen's calling cards announced that he 'Imports and Sells all sorts of Cambricks, Lawn, Macklin and English Lace and Edging, Where all Merchants, Dealers and Others may be Furnish'd, Wholefale or Retail at Reasonable Rates'.

Blackwork embroidery was usually worked with black silk thread. Little silk production was known in England before the seventeenth century and, therefore, the most sought-after thread had previously been imported from the eastern Mediterranean via the

Netherlands. Silk was so highly prized that in 1511 it headed the list of commodities exchanged for British cloth. Cheaper, undyed silks were also available on the English market, and embroiderers could make up their own dyes at home: until the regular supply from northern America of logwood, from the West Indian tree *Haematoxylon campechianum*, black dyes were prepared from tannins of oak galls or sumac and from salts of iron. Many of these dyes were not colour fast (the first system of controlled testing of fastness of textile dyes was not introduced until 1729) and much 'blackwork' has now become brown.

Black silk thread was relieved, or embellished, with metal threads, usually in the form of 'silver–gilt' or 'vermeil', as found in church and many other fine flat-work pieces in the Middle Ages and the Renaissance. Silver–gilt thread was composed of silver wire finely coated with a film of gold and either cut into strips which were subsequently wrapped around yellow silk threads or, alternatively, crimped or spiralled around a special screw or spiralling device to make a tubular cord.

Spangles, or sequins, often of sheets of silver–gilt cut into small roundels with central holes for retaining stitches, had been introduced to western Europe from Italy. Venetian ladies had used obsolete zecchino coins as costume decoration, and the fashion soon spread; although it was stated categorically by the then Master of the Gold and Silver Wyre-Drawers, Horace Stewart, in 1888 that the first reference to 'spangles' was in one of the *Wardrobe Accounts of Henry VIII*, it has in fact been ascertained that the *Wardrobe Accounts of Edward IV* for 1480 includes a description of the king's horse's trapping as 'an hoby harneis of grene velvett embrowdered and wroght with ageletts of silver and gilt and spangles of silver and gilt'. For later blackwork purposes, spangles were held in place with black silk retaining stitches, or they could be held with silver–gilt thread worked in knots such as a conical 'French knot'.

There is a very sophisticated blackwork panel in an upper gallery at Parham Park in Sussex. This embroidery, 18 cm × 126 cm (7 in × 49½ in), consists of individual blackwork motifs embroidered and then applied to a ground of white silk, the whole garlanded in a border of folded ribbon. The applied devices include sheep, a lady with baskets of fruits and breads for sale, snails, a deer leaping from behind a tree, a cherry tree, roses, pears, carnations, caterpillars and lions.

Some of the devices in the Parham blackwork panel are similar to those in 'The Shepheard Buss' (figure 7), an embroidery worked circa 1600 and now in the Victoria and Albert Museum. Branches with pears and other delicious fruits appear to have been taken more or less directly from Claude Paradin's *Devises Heroïques*, first published in Lyon in 1557. The panel is named from the inscription above the central figure, a mourning shepherd who is surrounded by Latin and Italian mottoes and emblems, and a band of verse which reads:

> 'False CUPID withe misfortunes WHEEL hath wonded HAND and HEART who SIREN-like did LURE me withe LUTE and charmde HARP. The CUP of care and sorowes CROSS do clips mi STAR and SUN. Mi ROSE is blsted ad mi BONES lo DEATH inters in URN.'

The capitalized letters are represented in the inscription by devices. The inner, oval, inscription is in Italian and reads:

> 'Di di in di vo cangiando il pelo e il mio miserabile viso.'

Several of the figurative patterns are similar to some of those portrayed in the Oxburgh hangings, worked a few years before the Shepheard Buss panel by Bess of Hardwick and Mary Queen of Scots.

What is the story behind the Shepheard Buss panel? It has been suggested that the initials 'KB' may stand for 'Kalendrier des Bergers'. The symbolism of the flowers and fruits is less obscure. The 'rose' of the outer inscription was one of four 'typical English roses' of the late sixteenth century. The national flower was

> 'not only esteemed for his beauty, vertues, and his fragrant and odoriferous smell, but also because it is the honour and ornament of our English sceptre as by the conjunction appeareth in the unity of these two most royal houses of Lancaster and York, which pleasant flowers deserve the chiefest place in crownes and garlands'.

Roses were essential to the English gentleman's life, and to that of his lady. Rosewater was used for washing hands and dried roses provided fragrant smells in the house: they must, indeed, have had considerable use as a household deodorant for contemporary everyday smells must have been quite unbearable.

The rose, therefore, was associated with what was good about England. Much early blackwork embroidery includes devices that offer intriguing and worthwhile paths of study. To take one example of symbolism in blackwork, the pomegranate—so beloved of Catherine of Aragon and incorporated into her emblem—appears again and again in blackwork embroideries from all parts.

8. A pomegranate design charted from Plate LXVII of John Taylor's *The Needle's Excellency*, first published in 1536

The pomegranate (figure 8) was a pagan symbol of fertility and regeneration and could be traced to ancient Semitic peoples. Its original association was with Proserpine who returned every spring to regenerate the earth. In Christian art the symbolism of the pomegranate was traced to the temple of Solomon, who built his temple with pillar capitals decorated with 'pomegranates also above, over against the belly which was the network: and the pomegranates were two hundred in rows round about the other chapiter'. (1 Kings 7:20.) The baby Christ is often portrayed in paintings holding a pomegranate, symbol of His Resurrection, and Mary has a pomegranate as a symbol of chastity. Queen Catherine was not the only dignitary later to adopt the pomegranate as impresa. Both the Holy Roman Emperor Maximilian I (1459–1519) and Isabella of Portugal, wife of his grandson Charles V of Spain, were to adopt it.

Looking at outstanding blackwork embroideries like 'The Shepheard Buss' panel thus provides interest for far wider a horizon than that of the embroiderer alone. One of the greatest art collectors of recent times was Sir William Burrell (1862–1958), a polymath in his interests, although his main collection is outstanding for stained glass, painting, superb woven tapestries, carpets and embroideries—many of which are blackwork. Parts of the Burrell collection were presented to the City of Glasgow in 1944 and others were willed after his death (see London, Hayward Gallery, *Treasures from the Burrell Collection*, exhibition catalogue, 1975).

Where did all the designs come from that were incorporated by early English blackwork embroiderers when they worked their covers, hangings or costume accessories?

Book illustrations transposed particularly well to monochrome embroidery and sixteenth-century stitchers were not slow to pick up new designs. One of the first books was *A Neawe Treatys as cocernynge the excellency of the Nedleworecke Spanisshe stitche and Weavynge in the Frame*. It appeared circa 1530 and was published by P. Quentel. The first recorded pattern manual printed in England was published by a surgeon, Thomas Geminus, in 1548. Called *Moryssche and Damaschin renewed and encreased very profitable for Goldsmiths and Embroiderars,* it was especially useful for blackwork embroiderers who wanted to copy arabesque designs.

Some of the patterns that have been most copied through the ages are those published by Conrad Gesner in his four-volume series *Historia Animalium* first published in Zurich in 1554. Many of the 'Oxburgh panels', attributed to Mary Queen of Scots and Bess of Hardwick and now, beautifully restored by the Victoria and Albert Museum, returned to their permanent home at Oxburgh Hall in Norfolk, take their shaping direct from Gesner. And some contemporary embroiderers used such designs not—as did the Scottish queen—as templates for polychrome embroidery but, instead, for blackwork.

By the end of the sixteenth century there was a proliferation of pattern books available. Federico Vinciolo's *Singuliers et Nouveaux Pourtraits* first appeared in 1587. It was republished in unabridged form in 1909 under the title *I Singolari e nuovi Disegni per Lavori di Biancheria*, translated by Stanley Appelbaum, and has been subsequently re-issued *(Renaissance Patterns for Lace, Embroidery and Needlepoint*, Dover Pictorial Archives, 1971). Vinciolo was a Venetian designer working at the court of Henry II of France. Although primarily a lacemaker, many of his designs could easily be transposed into the counted-thread art of blackwork.

9a Blackwork panel, a 'rural scene' possibly telling the story of 'the Disobedient Prophet'. The embroidery is 47 cm × 64.8 cm (18½ in × 25½ in). *(The Burrell Collection, Glasgow Art Gallery and Museum)*

The same adaptability could be applied to many of the early seventeenth-century pattern books. Johannes Sibmacher's *Schön Neues Modelbuch*, published in Nuremburg in 1604, has been transposed to embroidery and another popular work was Crispin van de Passes's *Hortus Floridus* (1614).

One outstanding early seventeenth-century designer was Thomas Trevelyon. His *Miscelleny*, published in 1608, is now incomplete, with only 290 out of an original minimum of 327 folios remaining. Each folio measures 42.5 cm × 27.9 cm (16¾ in × 11 in) and copies of the *Miscelleny* have been catalogued by the Boies Penrose Library and the Folger Shakespeare Library in Washington D.C. Trevelyon's patterns are drawn in thick outline (see J. L. Nevinson, *The Embroidery Patterns of Thomas Trevelyon*, Walpole Society, vol. 41, 1968, p. 3). One of his designs (Boies Penrose, Ms.

9b A polychrome embroidery, contemporary with the Burrell piece, worked in tent stitch on a linen ground 31.7 cm × 40.6 cm (12½ in × 16 in).

No. 1616; Folger Shakespeare, Ms. No. 1608), for single flowers in squares, is very similar to a blackwork pillow in the Metropolitan Museum of Art (see New York, Metropolitan Museum of Art, *Bulletin*, vol. XXX, 1935, p. 82). The design shows honeysuckle and borage flowers in alternate rows.

A study of early English blackwork embroidery is a veritable horticulturalist's delight. Flowers and fruits abound in designs of so many of the extant pieces. Other herbal and floral books that provided designs to embroiderers included *The New Herball*, published by William Turner in 1568, and Gerard's *The Herball, or General Historie of Plantes* (1597). Such books would have offered inspiration for professional and amateur embroiderers alike. The Broderers' Company had been refounded by Elizabeth I in 1561 and, although its members were by constitution all men and all professionals, doubtless much of their method of complicated patterning was passed on to their lady friends and fellow—though amateur—embroiderers.

One Burrell collection blackwork embroidery shows a rural scene (figure 9a). It was originally thought that the story showed the prophet Balearn but another theory, substantiated by the Print Department of the British Museum, identifies it as the story of 'the Disobedient Prophet' from chapter 13 of the first book of Kings. The 'man of God' disobeyed his orders and took both food and drink and as punishment 'a lion met him by the way, and slew him: and his carcase was cast, in the way, and the ass stood by it, the lion also stood by the carcase'. (1 Kings 13:34.)

The National Library of Scotland possesses a small *Biblia Sacra* (A. Tornesium, Lyon, 1567) with illustrations by Bernard Salomon. It shows a similar lion, man and horse (ass). But the most fascinating thing about the Burrell blackwork is that it is so similar to a polychrome work in a private collection in Scotland. This piece (figure 9b) was included in the National Art Collections Fund Edinburgh exhibition, Needlework from Scottish Country Houses, 1966, and it was described in the catalogue (Item No. 15) thus:

> 'Panel. Several incidents, including a man fallen from his horse, apparently killed by a lion, and two travellers, a man and a woman discovering him. On the right of the river, a lady listens to a shepherd playing bagpipes. On a bridge is a dog following a man with a basket slung over his shoulder; regarding him is a fisherman seated on the river bank. Silk and wool on canvas. Fine tent stitch. English; late seventeenth century. $12\frac{1}{2}$ in × 16 in.'

The young man peeping from behind the tree and the shepherd playing the pipes have been taken from a book of French engravings *L'Astrée* published in 1607–28 with illustrations by Honoré d'Urfé (1567–1625) and described as 'a romance in a pastoral setting'. This polychrome canvaswork embroidery is very similar to the overall design of the Burrell blackwork. There are many small differences: the canvaswork has a second castle to the upper left of the centre and the lower left shepherd is asleep. It has only three birds flying overhead. But in most respects the design is the twin of the Burrell piece. Both are a delight of romance, of symbolism and of adventure.

Some of the devices in the outer border of the Burrell blackwork appear somewhat unrelated. The cheetah sitting resplendent on a hillock, forerunner of the 'terra firma' mounds of crewel embroideries, the bare-bosomed lady with a basket of apples, the parrot looking in typical cock-eyed fashion at the snail behind him, the camel staring fixedly at two wilting sunflowers—these are but a

10 Strapwork design on a panel 47.6 cm × 41.2 cm (18¾ in × 16¼ in). *(Metropolitan Museum of Art, Rogers Fund, 1935, No. 35.21.3)*

few of the exotic pictures culled from sources all over the world that have been incorporated with more 'English' patterns like little rabbits, oak leaves and snails.

One of the most popular repeating patterns found particularly in seventeenth-century blackwork embroideries is the 'strapwork' design, an intercoiled scroll often shaped like ribbon with decorated edges. This is well exemplified by a cloth (figure 10) in the Metropolitan Museum of Art, purchased in 1935 for the Rogers Fund. The design is worked mainly in buttonhole stitch with some detailing in closed herringbone stitch. The strapwork is particularly elaborate and the interstices are filled with grapes and flower motifs.

A study of English blackwork comes to an abrupt halt with the dawn of the eighteenth century. Embroiderers in all parts of the world began to turn towards colour. They continued many of the designs and patterns their mothers and grandmothers had used.

But the new generation of needlewomen wanted to give colour to their stitching and they relied for effect not so much on stark impact, as typified by blackwork, but more on subtle shading and coloration of canvaswork and other embroideries. Blackwork virtually became extinct. It was to remain in hibernation throughout the eighteenth and most of the nineteenth century.

Caulfeild and Sawards' gigantic *Dictionary of Needlework*, first published in 1882 with sections on such various forms of embroidery as fish-scale work and spaced braid stitching (a form of needlepoint lace), has no entry whatsoever for blackwork. The paragraph 'Spanish embroidery' begins: 'a modern work, and closely resembling darning on muslin'. Two more modern standard books on nineteenth-century embroidery, Santina A. Levey's *Discovering Embroidery of the 19th century* (1971) and Barbara Morris's *Victorian Embroidery* (1962), similarly ignore blackwork altogether.

11 Detail of a cushion cover, 64 cm (25½ in) square, embroidered in brown twisted silks on a linen ground by Mrs Arthur Newall of the Fisherton-de-la-Mere Industry. Early twentieth century. *(Embroiderers' Guild, No. 2079)*

Blackwork was not to be regenerated until the beginning of the twentieth century. Some of the most outstanding pieces of 'modern' English blackwork are in the portfolios of the Embroiderers' Guild in London. One particularly fascinating piece is a cushion cover (figure 11), embroidered in brown twisted silks on natural linen. It was given by Miss Alexander and it had been worked by Mrs Arthur Newall, instigator of the Fisherton-de-la-Mere Industry. Mrs Newall had been inspired by some pieces of Italian two-sided cross stitch embroidery collected by her husband before their marriage and in 1890 she started teaching a girl of fourteen how to embroider. From this beginning sprang a large and vital cottage industry: at her death in 1923 it was estimated that she employed some forty out-workers (see L. Carbutt, *Mrs. Arthur Newall and the Fisherton-de-la-Mere Industry, The Embroideress*, vols. 1, 2, 1923–5, p. 219). Mrs Newall had always been instrumental in teaching her workers high standards and in revitalizing traditional styles to new uses. She herself wrote that her workers had to have 'industry, perseverance, concentration, honesty . . . and patience'. Certainly she must have possessed considerable patience to be able to work some of the carefully balanced fillings in her brown silk monochrome cushion cover.

Another twentieth-century 'blackwork' example in the collection of the Embroiderers' Guild in London is equally of interest to embroidered art historians. It is an apron (figure 12a) worked by Louisa Pesel (1870–1947) who is immortalized in the annals of embroidery not only for her unique samplers of assorted embroidery stitches now housed in the Victoria and Albert Museum but also for her diverse works on designs from all over the world. The photograph shows a detail from the pocket of Mrs Pesel's apron with a charting taken from the embroidery (figure 12b). The original was worked in double-running stitch in black Sylko on a ground of orange hand-woven linen. It was highlighted with controlled and skilful use of occasional white embroidery, illustrating an earlier historical pointer that 'blackwork' has, in many cases, sometimes allowed restricted use of a second colour—or metal threads or spangles—as further embellishment.

English blackwork therefore arrives, in chronological sequence, at the embroidery of today. But in order to understand fully the variety of 'traditional' and 'creative' blackwork being worked by modern embroiderers it is necessary first to look at examples of monochrome embroidery in other parts of the world and also to relate the art of embroidery to other facets of decoration and life in general.

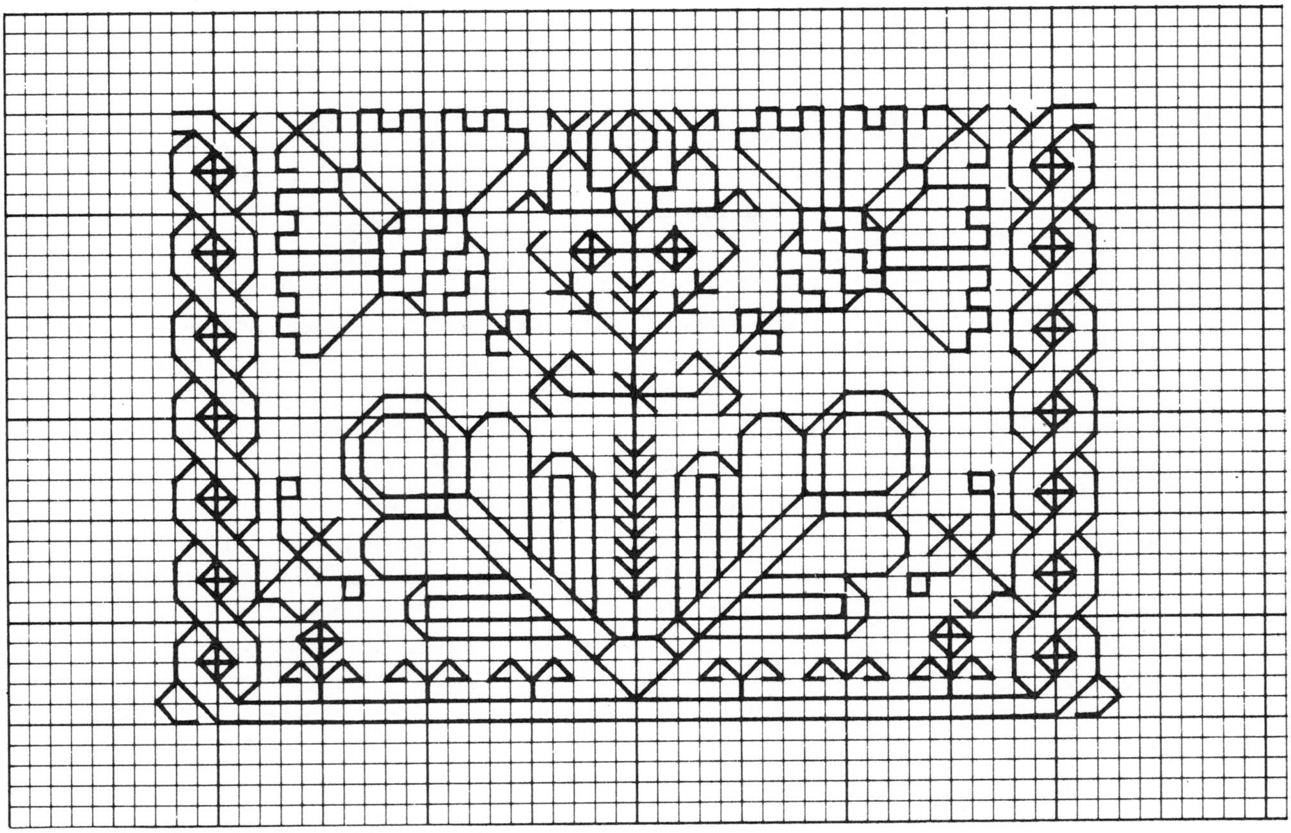

12a Detail of an apron embroidered by
Louisa Pesel (1870–1947).
(Embroiderers' Guild, No. 2080)
b Mrs Pesel had taken her design from a
sampler in the Victoria and Albert Museum
(No. 516–1877) and she reproduced it in
*Louisa Pesel's Historical Designs for
Embroidery* (Batsford, 1956, p. 48)

3 Blackwork of the World

American blackwork really came into its own in the nineteenth century, exactly when, in Engand, such monochrome embroidery was dormant.

In 1813 Hannah Poole of Westtown School in Chester County, Pennsylvania, worked a 35.6 cm × 27.9 cm (14 in × 11 in) sampler in black silks on linen. The inscription, in cross stitch, reads:
'Extract.
Fountain of being, teach us to devote
To thee each purpose, action, work and thought.
They grace our hope, thy love our only boast,
Be all distinctions in the Christian lost,
Be this in every state our wish alone,
Almighty, wide and good, Thy Will be done.'

Hannah Poole's homily is now in a private collection in Pennsylvania. Westtown was a boarding school, opened in Westtown Township, Chester County, on 6 May 1799 under the auspices of the Philadelphia Yearly Meeting of the Society of Friends. The girl students, all children of Friends, had to bring with them 'a pair of Scissors, Thread-case, Thimble, Work-bag and some plain sewing or knitting to begin with'. (Margaret B. Schiffer, *Historical Needlework of Pennsylvania*, Scribner, 1968, p. 44.) The girls spent two weeks of every six 'in the sewing school. Plain sewing comes first, and darning as well . . . this examination passed, the students undertake the complex embroidery of spectacle cases, gloves representing the earth, and samplers with beautifully stitched designs bordering alphabets and moral sentiments, usually in poetry'.

The blackwork results of such study can today accordingly be seen in many private and public collections. Westtown School still possesses one sampler, 30.5 cm × 26 cm (12 in × 10¼ in), worked in 1803 by Elizabeth Rowland in black silk cross stitch on a linen ground.

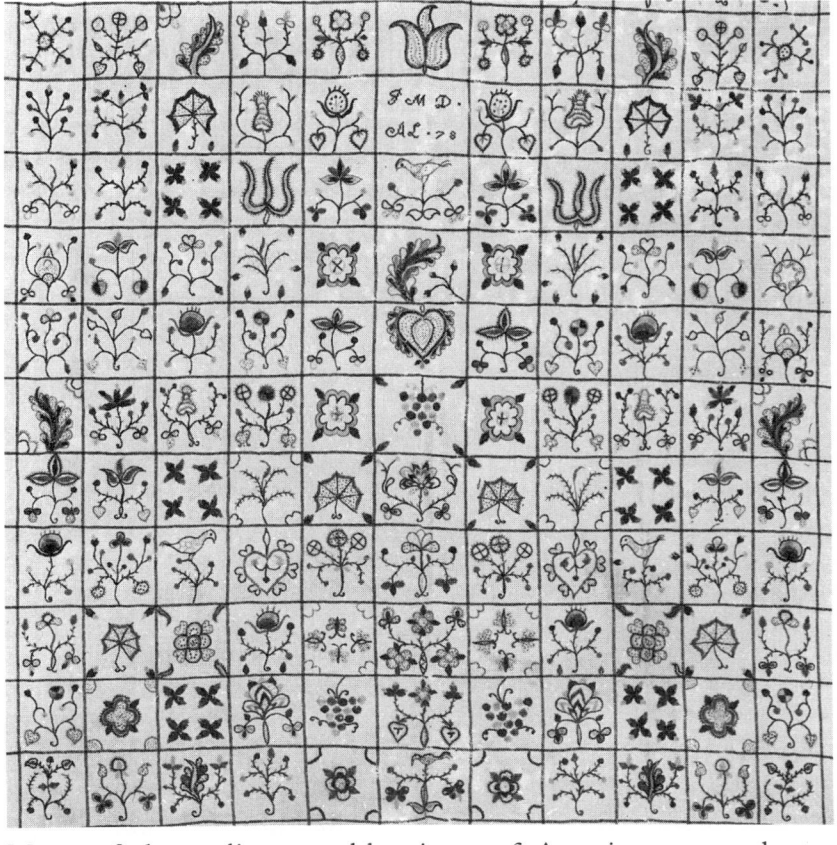

13 Embroidered bedcover, New York State, 1778. The design is executed in blue wool on a hand-woven woollen ground. *(Collections of Greenfield Village and the Henry Ford Museum, Dearborn, Michigan)*

Many of the earliest notable pieces of American monochrome embroidery were worked in blue on white, and as a rider to a survey of 'blackwork' it is worthwhile therefore to retrace the development of such one-colour stitching.

The designs for blue-on-white embroidery sometimes corresponded with those found on tiles and other decorative arts. A handwoven woollen bedcover (figure 13) in the collection of Greenfield Village and the Henry Ford Museum, Dearborn, illustrates how late eighteenth-century embroiderers had instilled a ceramic aspect to their work. The cover was initialled and dated 'S (?) MD/AL 78' and many of the 154 partitions are embroidered in crewel wools with patterns similar to Delft tiles. By the middle of the eighteenth century tin-glazed earthenware, originally from the Delft area near Rotterdam, had become popular in many parts of North America. If the Dearborn coverlet came from the area between Lakes Huron, Erie and Michigan, an area then, in 1778, still part of the North West Territory, it is quite possible that the design was in fact taken from imported Delft.

Similar blue-on-white decoration was later to be incorporated in 'Deerfield work', named after the town in western Massachusetts.

In 1896 Margaret Whiting and Ellen Miller, two unmarried ladies in their early thirties, decided to catalogue some of the traditional embroidery patterns that had long been used but had become recently neglected. Margaret Whiting had studied at the New York Academy of Design and Ellen Miller had been at Springfield. As well as practical laboratory-type examination of embroideries, dissection that often involved the unpicking of designs to see how they were made up, the two ladies also read diaries of prolific embroiderers like 'Aunt Bek' Dickinson (born Hatfield 1738), a needlewoman who embroidered many puzzle designs of unintelligible lettering, stitched in indigo thread. Miss Whiting and Miss Miller studied every clue they could find to establish historical design and thought. They looked at pieces of American crewel work and they delved into local animal and flower books to find out whence embroiderers of yore had gleaned inspiration. They published some of their findings in *Wild Flowers of the Northeastern States* (G. P. Putnam and Sons, 1895). And in 1896 they formed the 'Deerfield Society of Blue and White Needlework', so-called because blue was the most-used colour for their type of monochrome embroidery.

The Deerfield Society employed out-workers who were given stamped linen patterns, threads and small working drawings. Each piece was an original and the final stitches of each article were reserved for the society's logo, a small flax wheel enclosing a capital 'D'. The Deerfield Society continued functioning until it was disbanded in 1926: many of its embroideries can today be seen in the Deerfield Museum and a full account of its history has been given by Mrs Sheldon J. Howe in *Deerfield Blue and White Needlework* (published in the Needle and Bobbin Club, *Bulletin*, vol. 47, Nos. 1, 2, 1963, p. 42), and in *Deerfield Embroidery* (Scribner, 1975).

One of the earliest extant pieces of European 'blackwork' is the 'Kloster Adelhausen' funeral pall in the Augustinermuseum in Freiburg, Germany. The embroidery, dated the second half of the fifteenth century, is 294 cm × 158 cm (9 ft 7¾ in × 5 ft 2 in) overall and it is composed of three rows of five squares, each 50 cm × 58 cm (19½ in × 22   in), pieces of black cloth decorated with appliqué of white woollen twill cut in fine tracery. It is believed that originally this pall, which would have been placed prominently on a tomb around which processions were held, was further decorated with applied strips of gilt and silvered leather. The chiaroscuro effect achieved by the appliqué artists of the Kloster Adelhausen pall is similar to that employed by all 'blackwork' artists for it is, without exception, the *contrast* that is so important in all monochrome stitchery.

Religious usage of blackwork occurs in many parts of Europe. Sometimes, as in the case of the Kloster Adelhausen pall, the design of the black and white colour scheme itself provides sufficient pattern. In other examples the contrast of the monochrome design is skilfully employed to execute a more pictorial theme.

Anne Gøye's altar cloth (figure 14) is an example of sophisticated pictorial blackwork. It was worked in 1667 for St Peter's Church at Noestved and it is in reality an etched, engraved or printwork embroidery. The stitches are executed as if they were fine pen strokes. The cloth can now be seen in the Nationalmuseet in Copenhagen. The embroidery has five panels showing the Epiphany (the design for which was taken from the Piscator Bible, 1643 edition), the Last Supper (from Magdalena de Pas), the Crucifixion (from an engraving by K. van Mander de Gheyn) and the Women at the Tomb and the Ascension (both taken partly from Piscator).

A detail of the Epiphany panel shows the delicacy of the work. It is embroidered in outline blackwork stitching with controlled use of shading. The baby Christ is almost jovial as He looks up at the first of the Wise Men bringing in his gifts. Behind the Kings and their servants are two humorous looking camels and, in the distance, a heavenly scene that somehow looks rather like a portent of the tomb to come three decades later. As the attention of Mary and the Child turns to their new guests, shepherds and villagers make obeisance at the other side of the crib. The rafters in the stable behind them have a remarkably three-dimensional aspect, and the little details like the napkin in the basket in the foreground give an indication of the minutiae of the whole work.

A tour of monochrome embroideries of eastern Europe includes much work that is literally, as well as politically, 'redwork'. Red-on-white colouring is found in embroidery from many parts of the world but, principally, it is associated with eastern Europe.

When travelling through parts of Yugoslavia or Romania today it is still possible to see, in some rural areas, older women wearing brilliant red-on-white national costumes, with headscarves, blouses, aprons and sometimes skirts decorated with woven, applied or other embroidered patterns in bright scarlet. On Sundays and holidays many more people wear their traditional dress, and it is a lovely and refreshing sight, when driving along an international autoroute like that from Bucharest to Budapest, suddenly to come to a village with groups of ladies sitting by their front gates, each lady wearing a different patterned outfit and, possibly, herself embroidering both to while away the time and to produce something to sell to passing drivers.

14 A detail of Anne Gøye's altar cloth. The whole cloth is 178 cm × 290 cm (5 ft 10 in × 9 ft 6 in), worked in 1667 for St Peter's Church, Noestved. *(Nationalmuseet, Copenhagen)*

42

15 Sleeve panel on a late nineteenth-
century dress from Mrkonijíc Grad, West
Bosnia, 136 cm × 90 cm (53½ × 35½ in)
overall. *(National Museum, Sarajevo, No.
1663/1)*

16 Embroidered cuff, 5 cm × 14.3 cm (2
in × 5½ in). *(Embroiderers' Guild, No. 1235)*

In many instances the design of red-on-white embroidery runs parallel to true blackwork, as exemplified in a sleeve detail from a late nineteenth-centry dress (figure 15) overall, from the vicinity of Mrkonijíc Grad, West Bosnia. The dress, the property of the National Museum in Sarajevo, is worked in counted-thread patterns of stylized 'apples', 'branches' and 'small crosses'.

Sometimes the pattern on eastern European blackwork is more dense. A Balkan cuff (figure 16), embroidered in cross and buttonhole stitches, is more black than white. The cuff is in the collection of the Embroiderers' Guild.

One of the best collections of monochrome embroidery from eastern Europe is that to be seen today in the State Russian Museum in Leningrad. The embroideries in the decorative arts section are from all areas of Russia and elsewhere in the Soviet Union but a large part of the monochrome stitching is from the north of European Russia, from the Archangel and Vologda regions. Designs are worked in geometric or figurative forms, in shapes like the delightful Russian 'baba' (earth mother) variants, with squat ladies either riding on horseback or walking, alone or escorted by 'cavaliers'—one of the most amusing of all the patterns is indeed known as 'cavaliers and ladies'.

Russian towels, tablecloths and other household linens have often been decorated with monochrome embroidered panels. The Russian home has traditionally been enlivened with as much colourful stitching as possible and it is fun, and revealing, today to compare designs of pieces remaining in the Soviet Union, and on display in other museums as well as in the State Russian Museum in Leningrad, with those brought to the west either pre-1918 or by subsequent emigrés.

'Damascus goldwork' offers a relief of colouring. Gold-coloured, yellow or orange embroidery on natural coloured linen or cotton can today still be bought in the 'soukhs' (markets) of 'The Street Called Straight' and other areas of the Syrian capital, Damascus. Originally 'goldwork' was worked with damascene silk but today it is usually embroidered in two strands of standard embroidery thread.

'Damascus goldwork' can be found embellishing tablecloths, napkins, collars, cuffs and, also, marvellous smocks for men, the front tubes of the smocks held with fine pleated embroidery in back stitch, buttonhole stitch and with densely worked French knots. In some of the Druze areas, particularly the south of Syria, a similar form of goldwork embroidery can be found on men's clothing. But the gold-on-white colour scheme of monochrome embroidery is generally associated exclusively with Damascus.

Appliqué has already been included within the sheltering framework of 'embroidery' and it is therefore possible to include various topographical monochrome stitcheries such as a hat from the Cameroons. This piece, 33.6 cm (14 in) in height, from the collection of Mrs Clare Gebauer of Oregon, was included in the New York Museum of Modern Art's 1974 exhibition of African textiles. It illustrates the dramatic contrast of one colour applied to another. The same effect is achieved in another form of indigenous costume stitching from another continent, the 'mola' from the San Blas atolls of Panama. Although molas, panels for the front and back yokes of women's blouses and dresses, are usually formed of 'step appliqué' through many different coloured layers of cloth, some of the most effective of the patterns are those worked with one only different coloured layer of cloth laid on the original ground.

17 Cloth, 118 cm × 112 cm (46½ in × 44 in), embroidered in the 1922 textile class of the Kunstgewerbeschule, Zurich. (Collection of the Kunstgewerbemuseum at the *Museum Bellerive, Zurich, No. 218*)

One of the most prolific countries in the world of blackwork embroidery today is South Africa. Throughout the republic there are highly skilled groups working on intricate designs produced by such outstanding artists as Hetsie van Wyk, author of the definitive Afrikaans textbook *Borduur Só*. Any embroidery exhibition in the country is bound to include a large and important section devoted to blackwork and some of the tablecloths, handbags, cushions and other pieces produced represent the result literally of years of painstaking work.

Why is blackwork so popular today? One theory is that the architectural qualities of blackwork, with geometric calculations essential to eventual execution of a 'counted-thread' piece of embroidery, help instil a feeling of construction. Not only is the embroiderer producing a heritage for the future but she is also achieving a project that guarantees instant effect. No 'blackwork' can ever be described as inconsequential!

The construction element of blackwork can be illustrated with an example of Swiss blackwork. The embroidery (figure 17), worked in the 1922 textile class of the Kunstgewerbeschule in Zurich, has a pattern of scrolls, flowers on pedestals and borders of geometric squares. It is almost, but not quite, balanced. Swiss embroidery is traditionally thought of as being particularly delicate and intricate and this cloth, in the Museum Bellerive in Zurich, exemplifies the generalization.

Blackwork is, therefore, a positive and exciting form of embroidery. Taken in its most liberal meaning of 'one colour on one colour', it can be found in most areas of the world. And, as will be seen, embroiderers in England and in America, Australia, New Zealand, and in South Africa, are busily and creatively producing stitched pictures and other blackworks.

4 Artists' Blackwork

Holbein remains supreme among 'blackwork artists'. Double-running stitch is called Holbein stitch because of its close connection with so many of the painter's works, and it is true that many of the most outstanding portraits showing blackwork costume details are from his brush.

Hans Holbein the Younger (circa 1497–1543) was born in Augsburg into an artistic family. His father, Hans Holbein the Elder, was a skilled portrait painter who undoubtedly passed many of his techniques on to his son. After having served an apprenticeship in his father's studio and having learnt much, also, from the renowned Augsburg goldsmiths, the younger Holbein went to Basel in about 1514. He travelled extensively and came under the influence of Renaissance polymaths like Leonardo: it is, indeed, said that Holbein's 'Last Supper', now in Basel, owes much to Leonardo. Because of severe iconoclastic upheavals and strict censorship of the press, Holbein, armed with a letter of introduction from his patron Erasmus to Sir Thomas More, crossed to England in 1526.

His first English period lasted only two years. In 1528 he returned to Basel to work under a new regime but left again in 1532 to spend what were to prove to be the last eleven years of his life working in close association with the English court. He officially entered the service of Henry VIII in 1539.

It is estimated that Holbein executed about 150 portraits during the last decade of his life. At his death he left also more than 250 detailed designs for buttons, buckles and other costume accessories, horse-trappings and book-bindings.

His later portraits, which have been described as 'frozen, spaceless and impersonal', include many with details of blackwork. One of his last works, an oil on panel full-length portrait (figure 18) of Henry VIII, is now in the Walker Art Gallery in Liverpool. The king is standing with his legs apart and his arms akimbo, the better

47

18 Henry VIII by Hans Holbein (circa 1497–1543), oil on panel, 239 cm × 134.5 cm (94 in × 52 in). *(Walker Art Gallery, Liverpool)*

to display his gorgeous costume (was this too designed by his favourite, Holbein?). His doublet, with an above-the-knee skirt, is padded. It looks as if it is of white silk and it is decorated all over the bodice and sleeves, both of which are slit in typical mid-sixteenth-century fashion, with floral scrolls, borders of which extend vertically down the skirt and around the hem.

When different portraits of one subject by one painter are studied, blackwork (and other details) raise fascinating points of interest.

Another picture of Henry VIII, an 86.3 cm × 71 cm (34 in × 28 in) full-face portrait of the monarch clutching a staff in his left hand, shows Henry wearing the same shirt under a longer, closed, coat. He wears the same hat, although in this picture, in the collection of Hever Castle, Kent, it has been shorn of its fur trimming. In another, three-quarter face, portrait (figure 19) of the king, a painting in the Thyssen collection in Lugano, he also wears the same two forefinger rings as in the previous two paintings.

19 Another portrait of Henry VIII by Holbein. *(Thyssen-Bornemisza Collection, Lugano)*

Although the bodice of the Liverpool painting is front-opening that of the Lugano portrait looks as if the front is closed. The bodice slits are also larger and placed in three vertical lines. And the scrolled blackwork decoration has more entwining and less 'scroll'.

Five important versions exist of Holbein's portrait of Henry VIII's third wife, Jane Seymour. An engraving (figure 20) in the National Portrait Gallery is a copy of a painting in the Kunsthistorisches Museum, Vienna. It shows the queen wearing a chemise with cuffs frilled with blackwork embroidery. The floral design is enclosed in diagonal cartouches, a patterning that unifies the scroll of her slit sleeves with the geometric pattern of her oversleeves, and with the linear decoration of the two silk-covered bands covering her upper forehead and the undercap of her gable hood. The portrait has been described by the Director of the Gallery, Michael Levey, as 'superbly detailed but faintly flavourless—perhaps through some prim insipidity in the sitter'.

20 Jane Seymour, by Holbein. *(National Portrait Gallery)*

Other versions of the Jane Seymour portrait all show her in a similar stance, her hands clasped together. She wears the same basic robe but there is different detailing in each version. In the painting now in Mauritshuis, in The Hague, she has a simple necklace of pearls. She has no brocaded sleeves and her chemise cuffs have a simple floral blackwork border. The painting in the collection of Lord Sackville at Knole, Kent, shows a much more aged Jane, an interesting feature since all five paintings are dated circa 1536. The version in the collection of the Duke of Bedford at Woburn Abbey has no blackwork cuff decoration.

A test drawing for the Vienna portrait is in the Royal Collection at Windsor Castle (No. 12267). The 50.3 cm × 28.7 cm (19¾ in × 11¼ in) drawing is undoubtedly a pattern for the finished Vienna piece except for the fact that, in the sketch, Holbein worked only to the bottom of Queen Jane's hands.

The exquisite Royal Collection at Windsor contains many Holbein drawings with indications of blackwork embroidery that would be

21 Jane Lister, a drawing by Holbein on a ground 29 cm × 21 cm (11½ in × 8¼ in), in the Royal Collection at Windsor (No. 12219). *(Reproduced by gracious permission of Her Majesty the Queen)*

22 Holbein's drawing 11 in × 11 in (27.9 cm × 29.5 cm), of Lord Vaux which is in the Royal Collection at Windsor (No. 12245). *(Reproduced by gracious permission of Her Majesty the Queen)*

The Lady Lister.

better displayed in the finished portraits. A drawing (figure 21) of Jane, Lady Lister is executed in chalks and pen on pink priming. It shows Jane Lister, daughter of Ralph Shirley, a lesser official at the court of Henry VII. Jane was married first to Sir John Dawtrey and, subsequently, to Sir Richard Lister, who was appointed Lord Chief Justice in 1546.

Another Holbein 'blackwork' sketch (No. 12208) is of Simon George of Quocoute, a Gloucestershire gentleman, who was drawn by the master in chalks and Indian inks on a ground 28.1 cm × 19.3 cm (11 in × 7½ in). Holbein's drawing of Edward Clinton (or Fiennes), ninth Lord Clinton and first Earl of Lincoln (1512–84), a Lord-in-Waiting to Henry VIII at Boulogne and Calais, indicates the colouring of the eventual portrait. The sketch (No. 12198), 22.3 cm × 14.7 cm (8¾ in × 5¾ in), in chalks, silver point and pen on pale pink priming, is annotated with 'silb' (silver) and 'dofat' (taffeta) to show both colouring and intended texture. Similar indication of finished colouring is shown, too, in the drawing of the poet Thomas, second Baron Vaux of Harrowden (1510–56). This sketch (figure 22), in chalks and Indian inks on pale pink priming, is further illuminated with colour keys 'rot' (red) and 'w sam' (weiss sammet, possibly white velvet).

Holbein sketched his way throughout Henry VIII's court. A drawing of an unknown lady (Royal Collection, No. 12254), 27.9 cm × 19.5 cm (11 in × 7¾ in), has sometimes been thought to portray Anne Boleyn, Henry VIII's second wife, a lady whose regnum was brought unceremoniously to a halt when she was beheaded in 1536. Holbein subsequently painted Henry's fifth wife, Catherine Howard, who was queen from 1540–2. Her portrait, in the National Portrait Gallery, London, shows her wearing a braided underbodice puckering through the heavy slashes of her sleeves and with cuffs embroidered with blackwork scrolls. The painting is dated 1541. The following year Catherine, accused by Henry of adultery with a music teacher and, inter alia, with her cousin, Thomas Culpepper, was also beheaded.

Mary Tudor (1516–58) was the one surviving child of the marriage of Henry VIII and his first wife, Catherine of Aragon. She succeeded to the throne, as Mary I, in 1553. A portrait of her (figure 23), painted by an unknown artist circa 1554, shows her wearing the low cap or French hood that was high fashion from the 1520s to 1550s. Mary is known to have favoured a particular flat-crowned hood and in this painting, which used to hang in Hornby Castle, her cap is outlined with a halo of pearls and other precious stones. Her open collar reveals a garden of floral blackwork with a border 3.8 cm (1½ in) deep of daisy-type flowers. The collar is edged in buttonhole stitch and the whole design is remarkably simple and effective.

Many such blackwork patterns are, indeed, the more stunning for their simplicity. A portrait of Edward VI by Guillim Streetes shows the boy king, who ruled from 1547 to 1553, wearing an undershirt decorated with a mere hint of blackwork devices embellished with spangles and gold thread. This painting, 50 cm × 42 cm ($19\frac{3}{4}$ in × $16\frac{1}{2}$ in), is now at Anglesey Abbey, Cambridgeshire, in the collection of the Anglo-American art patron Huttleston Broughton, first Lord Fairhaven (1896–1966).

Mary Queen of Scots's half-brother, James Stewart, Earl of Moray (circa 1531–70) (figure 24), and his wife (figure 25), Agnes Keith, were both painted by the Flemish artist Hans Ewouts, known variously as Eworth, Jan Eeuwowts or Haunce Eottes. Ewouts (circa 1520–73), who came to England from Antwerp in about 1549, is sometimes referred to as a 'less substantial Holbein'. He

23 Mary Tudor (1516–58), painted by an unknown artist. *(National Portrait Gallery, No. 4980)*

laid great emphasis on the technical aspects of costume in his portraits and he delighted in the brilliant rendering of the richness of embroidery, brocade, jewels and goldwork. His are the initials 'HE' that are referred to constantly in the *Documents relating to the Revels in the Time of Queen Elizabeth* (Louvain, 1908). He is the designer who was called upon to plan masques, costumes and properties for Her Majesty's 'revels'.

His portraits are also calculatingly planned. His paintings of the Earl and Countess of Moray, both painted circa 1561, can be seen today in the Darnaway Castle collection, Moray. The Earl, 'The Regent Moray', wears a flat black cap and a black velvet coat with high upstanding collar edged with a narrow frilled linen ruff decorated with blackwork. The painting of the countess is 74.9 cm × 57.1 cm (29½ in × 22½ in) and it also shows blackwork embroidery on the delicate pie-frilled cuffs and a small upstanding ruff. It is quite possible that both these costume items were

24 James Stewart, Earl of Moray, by Hans Ewouts (circa 1520–83). *(The Earl of Moray)*

25 Ewouts' portrait, 74.9 cm × 57.1 cm (29½ in × 22½ in), of Agnes Keith, Countess of Moray. *(The Earl of Moray)*

26 'Lady in Green' by Agnolo Tori de
Cosimo Bronzino (1503–72). This painting
is 74.3 cm × 61.6 cm (29¼ in × 24½ in). *(Reproduced by gracious permission of Her
Majesty the Queen)*

imported, for it is sometimes suggested that although Mary Queen of Scots had herself left at Edinburgh Castle in 1578 'foure Inglis sarkes (chemises) with blak werk' there are no extant examples of *Scottish* blackwork: this theory is proffered by Margaret Swain in *Historical Needlework* (Barrie and Jenkins, 1970, p. 11).

Taking blackwork painters in chronological order of birth, one comes next to Agnolo Tori de Cosimo Bronzino (1503–72), an Italian painter most famous for cold, cultured portraits with a craftsmanship that has been compared with that of Ingres.

Bronzino's work set the tone for much court portraiture in Counter-Reformation England. Some of his most famous portraits can today be seen in the Uffizi Palace, Florence, and in the Metropolitan Museum in New York. One outstanding painting (figure 26), of particular interest to students of blackwork, is his 'Lady in Green', now in the Second Presence Chamber of Hampton Court. It is an oil painting, showing the subject with that cool analytical look associated with the artist. The lady wears an undershirt bordered with exactly placed blackwork motifs to either side of the front opening, on the cuffs and all over both the inside and the outside of the upstanding collar. Somehow the calculation that Bronzino put into his portraits has been extended to the chemise design. A similar 'blackwork' shirt is seen in Bronzino's portrait of Cosimo I de Medici, Duke of Tuscany, in the Pushkin Museum, Moscow.

The Metropolitan Museum of Art has a portrait (figure 27) of the French king Henri II (1519–59). It is an oil on canvas, transferred from wood, and it is from the workshop of François Clouet (circa 1510–72), a Fleming who worked in the international mannerist style promulgated by Italian artists during the period 1530–90. It is impossible accurately to assess what he himself actually painted and what was produced, to his design, in his workshop. The Metropolitan Museum's portrait has variously been attributed to the master (see Henri Bouchot, *Catalogue de l'Exposition de Primitifs Français*, 1904, no. 188; A. Weese, *Skulptur und Malerei in Frankreich*, 1917, p. 209) and also to his workshop (see Léon Palustre, *Album de l'Exposition Retrospective de Tours*, 1891, p. 13). One plausible compromise has been to suggest that it is a copy of a lost original by Clouet (see Louis Dimier, *L'Historie de la Peinture du Portrait en France au XVI Siècle,* vol. III, 1925, p. 128). At any rate, regardless of who did in fact paint the portrait in the Metropolitan Museum, the head is an exact copy of a Clouet original now in the Pitti Gallery in Florence. The blackwork student will note that the main embroidered interest in the portrait is in the decoration on the saddle cover.

An unknown French artist painted Sir Nicholas Throckmorton circa 1562. Sir Nicholas (1515–71) was an English diplomat who was Ambassador to France from 1560. The painting (figure 28), from the National Portrait Gallery, is now permanently displayed in the superb Long Gallery at Montacute House in Somerset, one of the finest of all Elizabethan houses, built in 1588–1601 by William Arnold for Edward Phelips. The combination of Tudor and Jacobean portraits now so appropriately displayed in the upper gallery of the house, a room with moulded plaster ceilings and with bay windows overlooking the surrounding countryside, is a masterstroke of planning. Sir Nicholas is portrayed in suitable diplomatic glory. Around the edge of his ruff and cuffs is heavy blackwork edging, possibly worked in buttonhole stitch.

The same blackwork edging to her gown can be seen in a portrait of Arabella Stuart now hanging at Hardwick Hall, Derbyshire. Arabella Stuart (1575–1615) was daughter of the Earl of Lennox and his wife Elizabeth Cavendish, herself daughter of that great embroiderer Bess of Hardwick. Arabella must have inherited some of her grandmother's fiery ambition. The painting, worked by an unknown artist when the subject was still a young girl, shows her with a determined expression. Arabella is known to have caused her grandmother continual worry and she later incurred the displeasure of her cousin, James I, by marrying William Seymour. She was sent to the Tower of London where she died insane.

27 Henri II, King of France, attributed to the workshop of François Clouet (circa 1510–72). This is an oil on canvas, transferred from wood, 156.2 cm × 134.6 cm (61½ in × 53 in). *(The Metropolitan Museum of Art, Bequest of Helen Hay Whitney, 1944, No. 45.128.12)*

28 Sir Nicholas Throckmorton, painted circa 1562 by an unknown artist. *(National Portrait Gallery)*

29a Sir Christopher Hatton, painted circa 1585 by an unknown artist. It measures 77.5 cm × 63.5 cm (30½ in × 25 in). *(National Portrait Gallery)*
b Design of the blackwork embroidery on Sir Christopher Hatton's collar and cuffs

30 Lady Kitson by George Gower, painted in 1573 when the subject was twenty-six. This is an oil on wood, 67.9 cm × 52 cm (26¾ in × 20½ in). *(Tate Gallery)*

Sir Christopher Hatton (1540–91) the dancing master, courtier and a favourite of Elizabeth I, was Lord Chancellor of England from 1589 to 1591. A portrait of him (figure 29a), painted circa 1585 by an unknown artist, is in the National Portrait Gallery collection at Montacute. The picture shows him, three-quarter face, holding a miniature in his right hand. His ruff and cuff are trimmed with needlepoint lace and with blackwork embroidery (figure 29b). The cuff embroidery shows a repeating pattern of zigzag or dog's tooth satin stitch blocking surmounting miniature scrolls and outlines of flowers and pomegranates 3.2 cm (1¼ in) in height.

The strength of many late sixteenth-century 'blackwork' portraits is well illustrated by some of the works of George Gower, an English gentleman known to have been undertaking commissions in London from 1570 to 1596.

Gower painted both Thomas Kitson (or Kytson) and his second wife, Elizabeth (1547–1628), daughter of Sir Thomas Cornwallis of Brome, Suffolk, who had been Comptroller of the Household to Queen Mary and Treasurer of Calais. The Kitsons undoubtedly were a family of substance and of personality: following a visit to their home, Hengrave Hall in Suffolk, in 1578, a visit described as with 'fare and banquet (which) did so far exceed a number of other places that it is worthy of mention . . . . A show representing the fayries as well as might be was there seen, in which a riche jewell was presented to the Queen's Highness', the Queen, Elizabeth, knighted her host. At one time he promised to comply with his sovereign's religious wishes but it is later recorded that Lady Kitson was subsequently imprisoned for refusing to attend Protestant services. But the Kitsons left their mark. Their elder daughter, Margaret, married Bess of Hardwick's son, Sir Charles Cavendish, in 1582 and the Kitson home, Hengrave Hall, built for Sir Thomas's father at a cost of £3,000 in 1525, is today an independent ecumenical centre.

Gower's portrait (figure 30) of Lady Kitson is in oil on wood and it was painted in 1573. It shows the subject (then twenty-six) wearing the exaggerated high-crowned hat that was adapted by Georgine de Courtais for an illustration of 'Elizabethan headwear' in *Women's Headdress and Hairstyles* (Batsford, 1973, p. 56). Lady Kitson wears a chemise and undersleeves embroidered with floral scrolls of blackwork and there is heavier stitching shown in the two fine lines around the cuffs.

Gower also painted Lady Kitson's youngest sister, Mary Cornwallis. She married William Bouchier, Earl of Bath, secretly at an unknown date. The marriage was annulled, apparently under

31 Gower's portrait of Lady Kitson's sister, Mary Cornwallis. This is an oil on panel, 117.2 cm × 94 cm (46 in × 37 in). *(City of Manchester Art Galleries)*

pressure from his family, and in 1583 the Earl married Elizabeth Russell, daughter of the 2nd Earl of Bedfrd.

Mary Cornwallis's portrait (figure 31), in oil on wood panel, is in the City of Manchester Art Galleries. It is one of the most popular 'blackwork' portraits and has been included in such scholarly surveys as Gertrude Townsend's *Notes on Embroidery in England during the Tudor and Stuart Periods* (1961). The coat-of-arms on the delicate rigid fan are those of her own family, the Cornwallises of Brome, and a painted miniature hangs from the bodice of her kirtle (full-length open tunic). The painting has been dated, from a contemporary bill, as 1573. Like her sister, Mary Cornwallis wears the fine gauze oversleeves later referred to by Ben Jonson (1572–1637) as 'shadow their glorie as the Milliner's wife doth her wrought stomacher with a smoakie lawne or a blacke cipress'. (Ben Jonson, *Every Man in His Humour*, act I, scene 2, lines 105–7.) Cipress (or 'cypress') was a sheer silk gauze. Under the oversleeves the full mainsleeves are decorated with blackwork embroidery in the form of an enormous sampler of oak leaves, lilies and roses, the motifs embroidered in many different forms of filling stitch and with some of the open flowers repeated, in simpler form, on the cuff frills. Her open gown reveals a panel of strapwork blackwork. The petticoat thus displayed underneath a full-length open kirtle is a forepart: in *Costume in the Drama of Shakespeare and his contemporaries* (Oxford, 1936), M. Channing Linthicum says that 'the Spanish kirtle needed a triangular accessory for the opening in the skirt. This accessory was known as a "forepart" ' (this definition contradicts a general assumption that a 'forepart' is a stomacher, to fill in a front bodice opening).

Apart from the costume details shown in the Cornwallis portrait, the painting is also of interest in that the elaborate patterning both of the sleeve embroidery and of the irregularly-shaped cartouches of forepart strapwork further identify this as a later—and more complicated—embroidery than others studied in this miscellany of blackwork portraits.

One of the most exact of all portrait painters in the 'blackwork' gallery is Marcus Gheeraerts the Younger (1561–1635), a Huguenot refugee and one of a closely interrelated group of artistic families. He himself married, in 1590, Magdalen de Critz, daughter of his stepmother, Susanne de Critz, second wife of Marcus Gheeraerts the Elder.

Gheeraerts the Younger was a portrait painter whose subjects are often shown 'in full sail'. His works have been described as 'full of half length, life-sized effigies of noblemen and women in full dress with heavy curtains, a table, or chair or a Turkey carpet as accessories' (*Dictionary of Art and Artists*, p. 169.) We see the curtain and table in his portrait of Mary Throckmorton, Lady Scudamore (National Portrait Gallery at Montacute). This oil on wood panel, 114.3 cm × 82.5 cm (45 in × 32½ in), is signed 12 March 1614. An inscription on the painting, 'No Spring Till now', relates to the marriage of her son John with Elizabeth Porter. Mary Throckmorton (died 1632), doubtless related to that earlier British Ambassador to France painted circa 1562 by an unknown artist, sits on a scarlet high-backed chair, the scarlet echoed in the red of her skirt and in the table cloth and curtain. Her open coat is of red and black brocade. Her collar and cuffs, of fine gauze, are liberally decorated with the same punto in aria (literally 'stitches in air'). Her bodice, which hangs over the skirt, and sleeves are embroidered with blackwork executed in the form of black silk laid in scrolls and couched with gold thread. There are spangles held in place with four radial black retaining stitches, there is black knot seeding or speckling and tiny groups, each about 1.3 cm (½ in) long, of duck's foot straight stitching. See inside front cover.

A slightly earlier—circa 1590—painting by Gheeraerts shows Captain Thomas Lee, a military man, described as 'an Elizabethan thug employed in the Irish Wars'. (E. K. Chambers, *Sir Henry Lee*, Oxford, 1936.) The 2.31 m × 1.5 m (7 ft 7¼ in × 59½ in) portrait, on loan to the Tate Gallery, shows Captain Lee barefoot, a surprising form of undress since the rest of his attire is extravagant, with blackwork floral patterns on his open shirt and sleeves. The painting echoes once again the general theme of Gheeraerts' attention to detail in a surrounding of strong furnishing items.

Once aware of blackwork, always aware of blackwork . . . continued study of paintings in galleries public and private brings forth new treasures in the search for monochrome embroidery details. A portrait of Isabella d'Este, Marchioness of Mantua (1474–1539), one of the most brilliant of the many cultured women of her time, shows her wearing a white chemise embroidered with red stitching. This painting, by Guilio Romano, in the collection of the Earl of Haddington, is similar to a version now at Hampton Court. In the latter painting, however, Isabella's chemise is plain and not decorated with blackwork (or 'redwork').

Sometimes only a hint of embroidered decoration is enough to tempt the blackwork student. Evidence of actual stitching—as opposed to weaving or printing—is accordingly occasionally in doubt. Does Titian's 'Venus and Cupid with Man Playing a Lute' (Fitzwilliam Museum, Cambridge), a marvellous pictorial work 152 cm × 196 cm (59$\frac{3}{4}$ in × 77 in), show the lute player with blackwork embroidery edging his narrow collar and cuff, or has the maestro merely put in extra shading?

5 Costume & Blackwork

The main period covered by blackwork costume is the century following 1530. And the most important blackwork items during this era were (for women) coifs and hoods, jackets (waistcoats), sleeves, stomachers, gloves, handkerchiefs and purses and (for men) nightcaps and shirts.

Until the sixteenth century the term 'coif' (or 'quaffe', 'quayffe', 'coyf' or 'quoft') referred to a man's close-fitting plain linen cap, rather like a baby's bonnet, with flaps to tie under the chin. By the sixteenth century, the original man's coif was worn only by a few learned professors and other generally elderly men. The new, contemporary, 'coif' referred to a lady's undercap, sometimes curving forward over the ears (in which case the coif had 'cheeks and ears').

It has long been debated as to how the sixteenth-century lady married her coif with a forehead cloth, known as 'crosscloth'. Many sets of matching coif and crosscloth were decorated with the same blackwork—or similar—embroidery. How were they worn together? Fortunately two such related pieces were found stitched together (see *The Illustrated London News*, vol. 189, No. 1, 1936, p. 533). The article showed how the triangular forehead cloth was worn, when in public, tied tightly over the head, with the long side over the forehead and the point hanging down behind over the main coif cover. In private, the forehead cloth was reputed sometimes to be tied even more tightly in a effort to prevent wrinkles!

Coifs were sometimes given to ladies as presents. Queen Elizabeth is supposed to have received several exquisite examples as New Year presents and such items must, indeed, have been well received. Many of the coifs were elaborately embroidered.

The Metropolitan Museum of Art has a fine coif (figure 32a) from the collection of His Honor Irwin Untermyer. It is embroidered in black silks on linen in stem stitch, back stitch and cross stitch

32a Coif, last quarter of sixteenth century,
16.5 cm × 21.6 cm (6½ in × 9½ in) when
made up. *(Metropolitan Museum of Art, Gift
of Irwin Untermyer, 1964, No. 64.101.1236)*
b Detail of the embroidery, executed in
black silk stem stitch, back stitch and cross
stitch

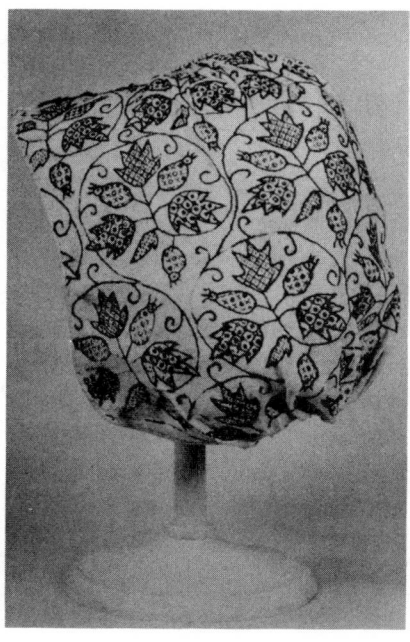

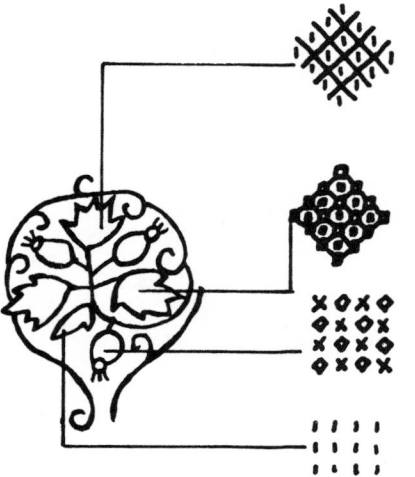

(figure 32b). It is dated to the last quarter of the sixteenth century and has been thoroughly documented by, inter alia, A. J. B. Wace (*English Embroideries Belonging to Sir John Carew Pole, Bart.*, Walpole Society, vol. XXI, 1932–3, pp. 56–7) and by Yvonne Hackenbroch (*English and Other Needlework Tapestries and Textiles in the Irwin Untermyer Collection*, Cambridge University Press, 1960, p. 5). The same design, of a branch with fruit and leaves displayed in a gently curving scroll, is found on a matching forehead cloth in the same museum. Close examination of one section of the design shows that the main leaf is diagonal trellis stitched with speckling (seeding worked in individual straight stitches) filling, the axillary leaves are trellised with boxed junctions and with blocked filling, the fruit (the pomegranate again) is worked in alternating crosses and diamonds and the small leaf to the bottom of the device is simply seeded throughout, with minute dot or running stitches.

The Carew Pole collection today constitutes one of the most outstanding private collections of examples of English embroideries of the last four hundred years. Select items from the collection, which has been handed down through generations of members of the Carew and Pole families, were included in the Lansdowne House Loan Exhibition of English Decorative Art held in London in 1929 and in the Metropolitan Museum of Art's exhibition, English Domestic Needlework of the XVI, XVII and XVIII Centuries, compiled by Preston Reminton in 1945.

There are many outstanding blackwork examples in the Carew Pole treasure-chest. Some pieces have been professionally mounted and glazed for protection. Other pieces have never been publicly displayed.

Two unfinished items deserve particular mention. One consists of a linen panel (figure 33) with the scrolled pattern originally pencilled in blue. Most of the design has been completed. The stitching was described by A. J. B. Wace in 1932 as 'coral stitch and chain stitch' but on closer inspection, in 1975, it was discovered that the main dark blue silk stitching has been executed in minute triangles of vertical straight stitches, with one 'long' (about 2 mm or $\frac{1}{16}$ in) stitch next to a medium stitch and in turn next to a 'small' stitch, another 'long' stitch and so on. Part of the finished blue embroidery has then been surface woven with metal thread. The metal threads have been worked in alternating links held only through the longest stitch of each trio of blue ground stitches. The metal chains are therefore entirely superficial and do not enter the basic ground fabric at all. The method of stitching is very complicated although the pencilled design on which it was worked is in essence relatively simple.

66

Another piece in the Carew Pole collection is a piece of linen (figure 34), part of which has now been cut away. It looks as if some of the design, a simple scroll, has been worked and it is this finished section which has been cut out. What remains has only partially been embroidered, in chain stitched silver-gilt thread.

Other coifs were embroidered in much more elaborate patterns. An unfinished coif (figure 35) in the Victoria and Albert Museum shows how a linen ground was printed with a design taken from an engraved plate. Only half the embroidery is completed. It was being worked in silks with silver–gilt and spangle highlighting. The pattern is a veritable paradise of flora and fauna and somehow its disregard of proportionate sizing only adds a delightful personal fragility to the whole piece. A squirrel is smaller than a strawberry. And the strawberries themselves are growing on a lily tree. Snails are climbing up rose trees and a pregnant monkey sits contentedly holding a ball. The more one studies this delightful unfinished coif the more fascinating the entire panorama becomes.

33 Linen panel, 44.5 cm × 26.6 cm (10½ in × 17½ in). The pattern for a coif has been partially completed. On a design in blue pencil, dark blue silk has been worked in straight stitches. Silver–gilt thread has then been superficially woven in and out of the blue stitches. *(Sir John Carew Pole)*

Contemplating items of blackwork costume can provide endless interest. The basic need for protection and warmth has long stimulated an art that is appealing to the designer, to the wearer and to today's student of costume. As the rapid expansion throughout the world of the study of costume continues, it is evident that appreciation is growing of the importance of fashionable clothing decoration to the age for which it was originally intended.

It has already been stressed how important the lilies, roses, carnations and pomegranates were to the sixteenth-century designer. Another coif (figure 36) in the Victoria and Albert Museum shows all these ubiquitous designs in its coiled pattern. What a delight it must have been for a lady to have had so appropriate a flower basket embroidered on her coif, with the design worked in plaited braid, back, chain and double-running stitches. This is a much heavier piece than the unfinished coif, and the black silk thread outlining is densely filled with silver–gilt threads.

34 Another unfinished coif, with part of the linen ground cut away. The original design measured 25.4 cm × 45.7 cm (10 in × 18 in) and it would have been executed in silver–gilt chain stitch. *(Sir John Carew Pole)*

68

The patterns of coif decoration depended to no small extent on the skill of the embroiderer. Doubtless pieces presented as royal, and other important, gifts were the work of professional embroiderers. Many extant coifs today portray a delightful air of the 'home' embroiderer. A coif and matching forehead cloth (figure 37) in the Middleton collection at the Castlegate Museum of Textiles, Nottingham, illustrates an element of amateur workmanship, although the embroiderer worked so patiently transposing a geometric pattern of fleur-de-lys with border partitions between each motif.

The Middleton collection contains many fine examples of blackwork embroidery. It is thought (see J. L. Nevinson, *Unrecorded Types of English Embroidery in the Collection of Lord Middleton, The Connoisseur,* January and March 1939, pp. 16, 136) that the outstanding costume pieces came from the collection originally accumulated at Wollaton Hall, built between 1580 and 1588 for Sir Francis Willoughby. It is amazing, and creditable, that somewhere someone, during the years, had the foresight not to dispose of so many exquisite and important items of sixteenth-century costume.

One of the finest Middleton blackwork pieces is a woman's hood

35 A more elaborate coif design, partially worked in plaited braid stitch, back stitch, chain stitch and double-running stitch. *(Victoria and Albert Museum, Crown Copyright, No. 21–1946)*

embroidered in black silks with rows of triple C-shaped leaves worked in buttonhole stitch. Such hoods, usually worn later in the sixteenth century by more elderly ladies, were descendents of the gable hoods worn by royal and fashionable ladies earlier in the century. Like the more usual coif, the sixteenth-century hood was also often elaborately decorated. There is a beautiful example (figure 38) in the Victoria and Albert Museum from the collection of the late Mrs Head, worked in stem stitch, double coral stitch and speckling with a pattern of honeysuckle, lilies and canterbury bells. It has an outer border of bobbin lace.

Ladies' jackets were also known as 'waistcoats' (or 'doublets') and they were in general use until 1625, after which date their usage was more or less confined to riding wear. The jacket was close-fitting and flared from the waist by means of gussets. It fastened down the front either with beribboned bows or with little buttons and the sleeves were sometimes held to the shoulders of the main bodice under protective 'wings', as seen in a jacket from the Isham collection from Lamport Hall, Northamptonshire. The jacket (figure 39), now in the Victoria and Albert Museum, is 44.5 cm (17½ in) in overall length. It is embroidered in silks on linen in

36 Coif with coiled pattern of roses, lilies and carnations. *(Victoria and Albert Museum, Crown Copyright, Collection of Mrs Grubbe, No. T.11–1948)*

stem stitch, braid stitch, back stitch and with speckling. The scrolled pattern shows pomegranates, roses, pansies and peapods, and it must have been gloriously effective when it was first embroidered, in the period 1610–30.

The Isham jacket has seen a certain amount of wear and, accordingly, the pattern has suffered. Fortunately other items of blackwork costume have been subjected to less constant pressure and the pattern therefore remains intact. A close-up detail (figure 40a) of a lady's jacket in Maidstone Museum, Kent, shows a monochrome design of red silk on white linen with stem stitch outline and fine speckling in-filling. The make-up of this jacket is considerably simplified, with the outer shoulder 'wings', so apparent in the Isham piece, here reduced to hardly discernible inset frills. The peapods and their foliage alone constitute a most effective decoration (figure 40b). The sweet pea (*Lathyrus odoratus*), an annual native to Italy, was by the sixteenth century popular throughout all parts of western Europe. It has alternating leaves, faithfully reproduced by the embroiderer of the Maidstone jacket,

37 Coif and matching forehead cloth in the Middleton Collection. *(Castlegate Museum of Textiles, Nottingham)*

who has worked to a natural sizing of hairy pods about 5 cm (2 in) in length.

The fashionable lady's decolletage was sometimes rather revealing. Modesty could be ensured through the wearing of a 'partlet' (or 'patlet'), a filling that sometimes, from circa 1530, even had its own standing collar. These partlets were often delicately edged with blackwork embroidery, sometimes designed to match the stitching on cuffs and sleeves. Embroidery was generally worked in a variety of repeating patterns, as shown in two pieces (figure 41) in the Victoria and Albert Museum, panels worked in dark brown silk on linen in back stitch, double-running stitch and speckling. These panels, which have lost a certain amount of the original stitching, illustrate the careful geometric proportioning that went into many of the blackwork costume items of the late sixteenth and early seventeenth centuries.

Geometric exactness is also a feature of the famous blackwork cape-collar (figure 42) in the Middleton collection (Castlegate Museum, Nottingham). The collar is similar to a plain white

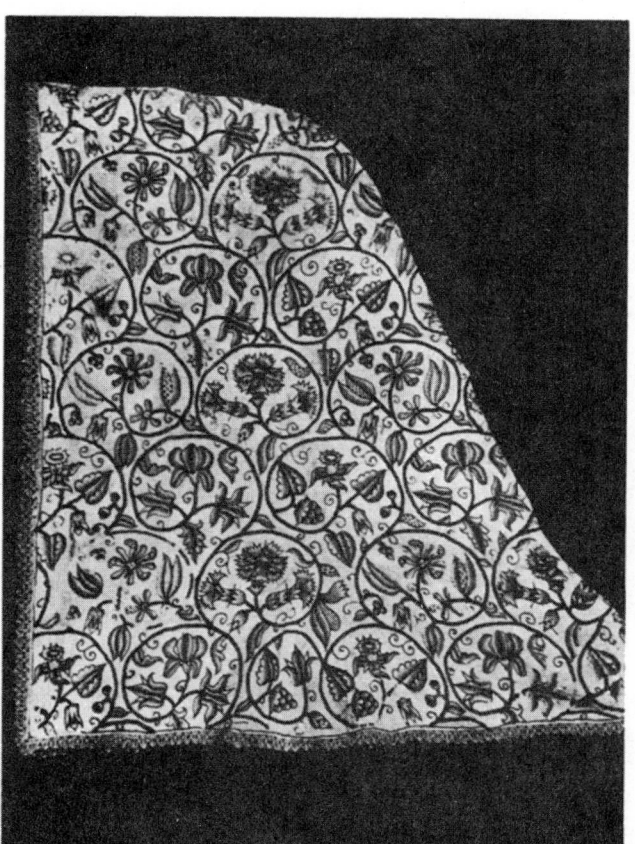

38 Woman's hood, 52 cm × 53.3 cm (20½ in × 21 in), embroidered in stem stitch, double coral stitch and speckling. *(Victoria and Albert Museum, Crown Copyright, No. T.135–1924)*

39 Linen jacket embroidered in black silk, 44.5 cm (17½ in) in length. *(Victoria and Albert Museum, Crown Copyright, No. T.4–1935)*

lacework double-falling cape-collar in the Filmer collection (Victoria and Albert Museum) and, also, to one shown in a portrait (at Welbeck Abbey) of Elizabeth Vernon, Countess of Southampton, painted circa 1580. Cape-collars were négligé coverings for the shoulders and were worn whilst dressing—much as in the same way, today, ladies sometimes wear plastic or nylon shoulder covers to protect themselves from hairspray and face powder. The Middleton cape-collar is embroidered in black herringbone stitch and it has an interlaced scrolling design (figure 42b) It is edged with bobbin lace.

Toilet apparel for both ladies and gentlemen often contained blackwork items. The Carew Pole collection used to include a

40a A peapod design on a woman's jacket embroidered in red silk on a linen ground. *(Maidstone Museum and Art Gallery)*
b Another peapod design, drawn from a late seventeenth-century blackwork cloth.

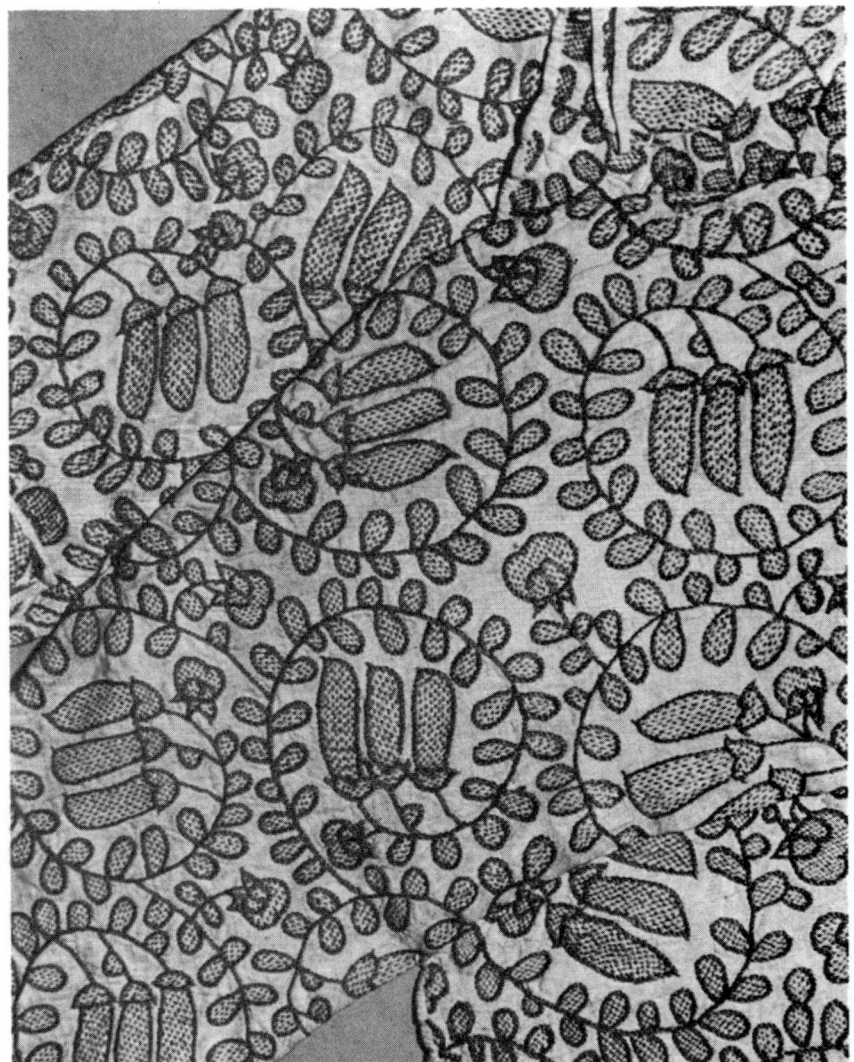

handkerchief with a blackwork border of flowers and fruits embroidered in oriental and coral stitches with buttonhole and speckling filling. The handkerchief, 40.6 cm × 38.1 cm (16 in × 15 in), was initialled 'PE' for Peter Edgecumbe (1536–1607), a gentleman whose sister Elizabeth had married Thomas Carew. The handkerchief was, alas, reported missing in 1948 and its whereabouts are not now known.

As with the coif, the handkerchief was often given as a New Year's present. John Nichols (*The Progresses of Queen Elizabeth,* London, 1723) refers to various blackwork handkerchiefs given to Her Majesty:

'1578–9 from Lady Digby:

'6 fair handkerchers of camerik of black Spanish work, edged with a border of bone lace of gold and silver"

41 Two costume panels, embroidered in dark brown silk in back stitch and double-running stitch. *(Victoria and Albert Museum, Crown Copyright, No. T.14–1948)*

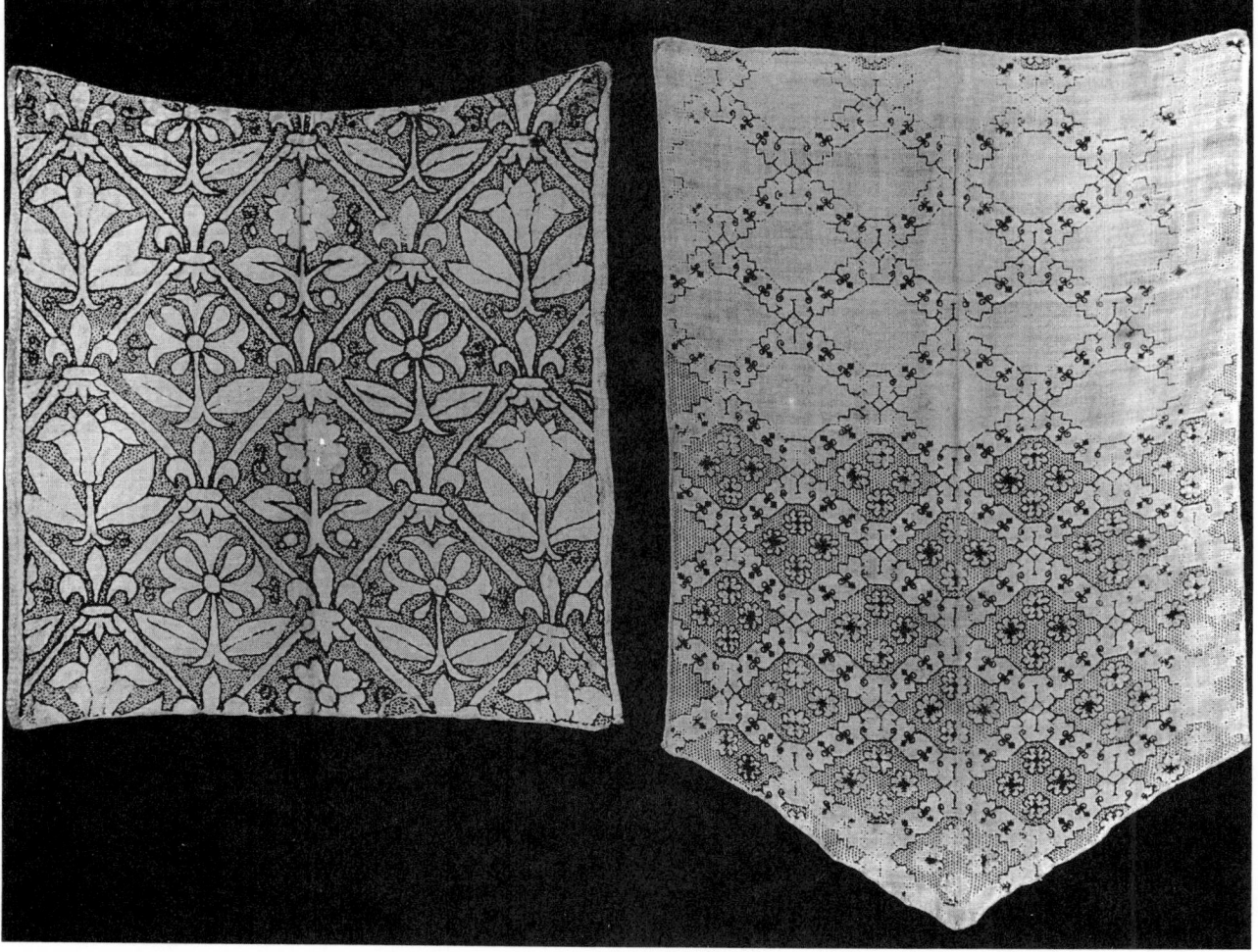

42a The famous 'double-frilled' cape-collar in the Middleton collection, 52 cm × 64.8 cm (20½ in × 25 in) overall. *(Castlegate Museum of Textiles, Nottingham)*
b Detail of the scroll pattern on the cape-collar

1588–9 from Mrs Smithson:
"2 handkerchers of Holland wrought with black silk"
1599–1600 from the Countess of Kent:
"6 handkerchers of cambricke, wrought with black silk and edged about with gold lace".'

There is a fine handkerchief (figure 43) with monogram in the Burrell collection (Glasgow Art Gallery and Museum), with a repeating design around the edges. The design is more or less symmetrical, taking an axis from the initialled corner diagonally across the cloth. Each of the motifs shows a device taken from a carnation, ubiquitous in embroideries of the sixteenth and succeeding centuries. The carnation, known variously as the 'geliflower' (*La Clef des Champs*, Jaques le Moyne's 1586 flower book) and the 'gilliflower', was so universally popular that William Lawson, a Yorkshire gardener who lived at the beginning of the seventeenth century, wrote that they were 'of all flowers (save the damask rose) the most pleasant in sight and smell'. The Burrell handkerchief has carnations that look distinctly eastern Mediterranean, or eastern European, in style.

Although most of the handkerchiefs in existence today were worked

43 Handkerchief, 38.1 cm × 35.6 cm (15 in × 14 in), worked with monogram. *(The Burrell Collection, Glasgow Art Gallery and Museum)*

in England or western Europe, a few outstanding pieces survive from the rest of the world. There is a 45 cm × 40 cm (17¾ in × 16½ in) example now in the Moravian Museum in Brno. The handkerchief is worked in red silks on a linen ground, the design worked mainly in cross stitch and back stitch. It is dated 1560, the year outlined in back stitch crudely worked above a central pattern of a lady, with a marvellous feathered cap, and a gentleman, like his lady full-skirted and with similar headwear. The lady holds a flower, her cavalier a tall vase or double cup. The couple is worked in cross stitch. To either side are outline motifs of a bird surmounting a heart and a double flare. The greater part of the ground of the handkerchief is left unworked but each corner has a dense border design with inner arabesque. This handkerchief could equally have been carried by a lady or a man. What about gentlemen and blackwork costume in general?

Some of the most superb of all 'masculine' blackwork items are nightcaps, part of the at-home dress of the fashionable English gentleman. They were worn, despite their name, during the day: the operative *night*cap was a sleeping cap, the 'biggin' as mentioned in Shakespeare's *King Henry IV* (1597): 'As he whose brow the homely biggin bound snores out the watch of night.' The (daytime) nightcap, usually with upturned brim, was a relief from the customary wigs and more formal headgear of public wear, and they were worn by men of all ages. One William Freke, a student at Oxford, is reputed to have paid 17s 6d in 1629 for a 'blackwork and gold cappe' (see M. Channing Linthicum, *Costume in the Drama of Shakespeare and his Contemporaries*, Oxford University Press, 1936, p. 150). Caps were sometimes elaborately embroidered. The 1583 inventory of Kenilworth Castle (Mss. of Robert Dudley, Earl of Leicester, Historical Mss. Commission, London, 1925) includes 'three double nighte cappes of hollande, edged and wroughte about the brymmes with black silk'.

Many gentlemen did not look after their nightcaps with great care. There is a cap in the Royal Ontario Museum, Toronto (No. 973.162.1) that shows evidence of the cap having seen considerable wear. The piece was given by Mrs Edgar J. Stone in memory of Harold Burnham and one of its main points of interest is that it does illustrate very effectively the construction of such items of headwear. The crown was made of one piece, divided into quarters at the top to produce the shaping. Sometimes the rim was also formed from the same piece of fabric, embroidered on the reverse side of the fabric from the crown. The construction of a cap is most effectively illustrated by a superb piece (figure 44) in the Carew Pole collection. On a fine linen ground a pattern has been worked in green silks in a curling feathered design. The top of the pattern has been divided into four segments. And the bottom horizontal band is worked on the reverse, thus to form, when made up, the upturned brim. Only one of the four crown segments has been finished: it has metal thread highlighting to the green silk monochrome patterning.

There are two outstanding finished nightcaps in the same collection. One (figure 45) is worked in stem stitch with plaited work. The crown seams have come undone since the cap was worked in the late sixteenth century. The other cap, possibly the more distinguished of the pair, is contemporary and was worked in stem stitch, chain stitch and with speckling. It is 19.7cm × 53.2 cm (7¾ in × 21 in) opened up, and was shown in the 1929 Lansdowne House exhibition (No. 213). The speckling of this cap is fairly substantial in appearance. The cap has been designed for masculine appeal. The same element of definite design is seen in another cap (figure 46) (Burrell collection, Glasgow Art Gallery and Museum). This piece is worked in black silk with gold metal highlighting.

Men's caps could thus be designed with the wearer in mind. But,

44 An unfinished 'nightcap' showing how the pattern would form four quarters of the upper crown of the cap. The bottom of the cap would be turned up to form a brim. It measured 25.4 cm × 53.3 cm (10 in × 21 in). The embroidery was worked in green silks. *(Sir John Carew Pole)*

45 Nightcap embroidered in stem stitch and plaited stitch, 20.3 cm × 26.6 cm (8 in × 10½ in). *(Sir John Carew Pole)*

46 A masculine design for a gentleman's cap, 21.6 cm × 27.3 cm (8½ in × 10¾ in). *(The Burrell Collection, Glasgow Art Gallery and Museum)*

since nightcaps were 'at home' apparel, it is not surprising that some items were decorated with designs that would have been more appealing to the beholder. There is a much lighter design to be seen on a nightcap (figure 47) in the Zouche collection at the Victoria and Albert Museum. It is also dated late sixteenth century, worked in silk and silver–gilt threads on linen with long-and-short and herringbone stitches. The scrolled pattern shows acorns, carnations, roses, holly and peapods.

Did Sir Thomas More (1477–1535) ever wear the nightcap sometimes attributed to his ownership? The cap is now in the collection of Stonyhurst College, Lancashire, and it has been described variously as 'the cap he (Sir Thomas More) wore to the last' and a 'skullcap'. Whatever its origin, the cap is 20.3 cm × 25.4 cm (8 in × 10 in), linen embroidered in 'monochrome' stitching of silver wire, with a loosely fitting, narrow, lace-like circlet of gold wire and spangles.

After the heyday of blackwork in costume, a period which lasted until about 1630, there is a noticeable void in general use of this form of decoration until the twentieth century.

Today, fortunately, the striking effect of black-with-white is being revived by designers. Sir Cecil Beaton had already made an impact with his 'Ascot' designs for the film of 'My Fair Lady' and in 1971, in his exhibition, Fashion, at the Victoria and Albert Museum, he again showed black-on-white in some of the pieces he culled for this personal show.

Item No. 149 in the 1971 Beaton exhibition was a 1969 design by Madame Grès, the former French sculptor later best known for her skilful and subtle use of jersey and other haute couture fabrics. In this dress (No. 177), Grès cut a rectangle of bucol with an opening for neck and arms. In wear, the dress falls with one shoulder bare, sweeping sideways into a dramatic asymmetrical drape. The dress was worn by Mrs Graham Mattison and later presented by her to the Victoria and Albert, where it can be seen in the main Costume Court (No. 5).

47 Sometimes nightcaps were designed
with less masculine a pattern. This example
has a lighter design and measures 19.7
cm × 26.7 cm (7¾ in × 10½ in). *(Victoria and
Albert Museum, Crown Copyright, No.
T.814–1891)*

6 Techniques for Blackwork

Before delving into some of the mystique surrounding blackwork of yesterday and adapting the tricks of our ancestors to embroidery of today, it is necessary to make sure that the right equipment is to hand.

NEEDLES

A tapestry needle with a blunt end is preferable. It is essential that the needle slides between—rather than splitting—the threads of the ground fabric.

GROUND FABRIC

A counted-thread blackwork embroidery depends for much of its final effect on the ratio of stitches to centimetre, or inch, of the ground fabric. The higher the number of warp and weft threads to the centimetre and inch, the smaller—and more dense—the ultimate pattern. This is illustrated by two pieces (figure 48) in the collection of the Embroiderers' Guild. Both dragons were worked in 1955 by Elisabeth Geddes. She adapted her design from a booklet produced by the Needlework Development Scheme and worked more or less the same pattern (there are a few incongruities in the working of the tail, front claws and other addenda) on two pieces of fabric, one 11.4 cm × 15.2 cm (4½ in × 6 in) and the other 13.9 cm × 20.3 cm (5½ in × 8 in). The different 'scale' of the finished embroidery depends, as is shown, on the sizing of the mesh of the ground fabric. This is known as the 'thread count', the number of warp and weft threads to the count, usually of five centimetres or of one inch.

The chosen thread count depends to some extent on the eyesight of the embroiderer. Blackwork, particularly fine counted-thread work, is a taxing form of embroidery and can be tiring to the eyes. It is therefore sometimes a good idea to begin blackwork with a fairly low thread count, on a 'wide mesh' fabric.

48 Two embroideries by Elisabeth Geddes. The upper piece is 11.4 cm × 15.2 cm (4½ in × 6 in), the other 13.9 cm × 20.3 cm (5½ in × 8 in), and they illustrate how the eventual size is governed by mesh of ground fabric. *(Embroiderers' Guild, No. 929)*

A slub fabric, with some warp or weft threads varying slightly in thickness, can give added variety to blackwork embroidery, but it is generally preferable to begin with an evenweave fabric with usual weave (one warp and one weft thread) or on a double (Hardanger) weave (two weft threads woven together under and over two warp threads).

Supplies of evenweave linens and cottons depend very much on what needlework and art supply shops have in current stock. In order to be completely up to date with new fabrics available it is a good idea to call on a local stockist (see list p. 156) or to write to one of those concerns that offers mail business and ask for swatches of what is recommended for blackwork.

Some of the most popular ground fabrics for blackwork embroidery today are included in the following table.

Ground fabric	Approximate thread count per		Width
	5 cm	1 in	
'Glenshee' evenweave linen (100% flax) recommended in ivory, natural, cream	56	28	55 cm (22 in) and 132 cm (52 in)
'Glenshee' linen recommended in natural and oatmeal	37	18	35 cm (14 in), 45 cm (18 in), 55 cm (22 in) and 127 cm (50 in)
'S.P.' evenweave linen recommended in ivory	52	25	55 cm (22 in) and 127 cm (50 in)
'Needlewoman' evenweave linens in assorted thread counts recommended in ivory	38	19	137 (54 in) to 150 (59 in)
	42	21	
	52	26	
	60	30	
	68	34	

There is also a variety of linen scrim, evenweave cotton and man-made fibres, Penelope, Hardanger and 'Danish' fabrics, as available from the recommended stockists.

EMBROIDERY THREAD

It is often said that the thickness of the working thread should not be dissimilar to that of the threads in the ground fabric, but since it is partly the relationship of embroidery thread to ground fabric that constitutes the chiaroscuro of eventual effect it is impossible to generalize on which thread should be married to which partner.

It is possible to dogmatize that *single* threads should be used throughout. In order to get as even a working result as possible, it is necessary to use only *one* strand of embroidery yarn. Two or more strands twist, clog up and do not work evenly. It is better to change to a thicker one strand of thread if a more dense colouring is suddenly required.

Some of the threads recommended for blackwork embroidery today include the following.

Soie perlé, real French silk, available in 16 metre (17 yard) spools or 80 metre (87 yard) spools, an expensive 'luxury' thread that is difficult to get hold of.

Soie d'Alger, again real French silk, sold in skeins by weight.

D.M.C. 'coton perlé', 'à broder' and 'mouliné spécial' in assorted thicknesses, sold in skeins.

Pearsalls, 'twisted' embroidery silk, sold on cards.

Clark's, 'anchor' thread, sold by skein.

Ordinary sewing thread, for either hand or machine sewing.

As with the embroidery fabric, it is a good idea to contact one's favourite 'supplier' and see what he, or she, recommends as the best thread for the particular fabric in stock.

METAL THREADS

The usual metal threads for blackwork today are lurex, 'Jap gold' and 'purl thread' (or bullion). Lurex, most used of all synthetic threads, is easy to handle, is pliable to work with and does not tarnish. Fine lurex threads can be stitched right through the ground fabric.

'Jap gold', available in various sizes, is made from wafer-thin narrow strips of pure gold coiled around a silk floss thread. 'Purl thread' (or bullion) is coiled metal thread without the central thread found in 'Jap gold'. 'Purl' comes in various forms: rough (or matte) purl, a dull satin sheen; smooth (or glissant) purl, very shiny finish; check purl, chequered, sparkling finish; pearl purl (or wire or badge purl), the kind of purl used for blazer badges and similar heavy pieces. Both 'Jap gold' and 'purl' must be carefully worked. They should be manipulated with tweezers and not man-handled unless absolutely necessary. More amenable, from an operative viewpoint, is the new synthetic thread now available under various names (it can be called 'Jap gold substitute' or 'new quality imitation gold thread' depending on the stockist). It comes in 18 metre (20 yard) spools in various sizes.

To recapitulate, selection of all ground fabrics and embroidery threads depends on what the stockists have available and, also, on what the embroiderer needs for a particular project. It is always a good idea to have a 'friendly stockist' and, apart from the list of those recommended in this book, there are names of suppliers in all good embroidery magazines and similar periodicals. With the increasing interest in embroidery in many parts of the world, new embroidery shops and stockists are opening up with every month. The only difficulty with dealing with a mail-order stockist is that it is sometimes necessary to order supplies in plenty of time before a project is started. This advance organization is particularly important for embroiderers wishing to have supplies sent by surface mail from one country to another.

OTHER EQUIPMENT

Apart from the usual needlework paraphernalia of scissors, thread-unpicker (essential for rectifying the initial mistakes that some-times even the most skilled mathematician and geometric embroiderer makes from time to time), blackwork embroidery may require the following trappings: an embroidery frame for holding the fabric taut (either a free-standing hand-held frame or a frame fixed to chair or floor can be used—a cheap alternative is to use artists' frames, lengths of wood of assorted lengths that slot together very easily); a free-standing (or neck-hanging) large-scale magnifier, preferably an electrically illuminated magnifier that provides plenty of light for the embroiderer (this is very useful when working a particularly high-density pattern); graph paper, pencils, rulers, erasers and other artists' essentials (for trans-position of design).

STITCHES

And now with all equipment literally to hand—or hands—it is time to begin. Before attempting to transpose an original design into blackwork embroidery, it is sometimes a good idea to work an initial sampler of some of the more well-known 'historical blackwork' stitches. These include the following stitches.

Back stitch
Braid stitch
Buttonhole (blanket) stitch.
Chain stitch.
Coral stitch.
Double-running (or Holbein) stitch.
Herringbone stitch.
Pekinese stitch.
Speckling (or seeding).

The methods of working these stitches is still the same today. Figure 49 shows the main stages for each stitch.

Back stitch is known variously as 'point de sable' and 'stitching'. The basic stitch can be crossed, ringed, whipped or worked in two parallel lines, working alternately from one line to another with the thread forming a cross behind. 'Ringed back stitch', with lines of stitching forming joined links of chains, is also known as 'festoon stitch'. The variety of back stitches is endless and once the main basic stitch is mastered, many useful 'blackwork embroidery' stitches become available. The main essential with back stitch is that the needle always goes back into the ground fabric at the end of the last stitch, always therefore completing a stitch before beginning a new one.

Braid stitch is a more complicated 'scroll-type' stitch. It is worked, as in the diagram, from right to left (for a right-handed embroiderer) and it produces a line of scrolls that, when complete, looks like the kind of braid that can be bought for dressmaking or furnishing requirements. It is difficult for the blackwork beginner to achieve even working in a line of braid stitch. This stitch, more than some of the other more-usual 'historical blackwork' stitches, therefore demands sampler, or test, working before being put on to a piece of creative blackwork embroidery.

Buttonhole stitch, or 'blanket stitch', need not necessarily be the edging stitch that its name so implies. Some of the most effective uses of buttonhole stitch are when it is executed as a filling stitch, either spaced or closed, with one line of stitches joining a line above or below. Buttonhole stitch can be worked with pairs of stitches forming triangles or forming crosses. And each individual stitch can be knotted to produce a more complex final patterning.

Chain stitch is one of the most versatile of all basic embroidery stitches. The linked chains, with the needle always going back into the ground fabric inside the penultimate link, have lent themselves to blackwork embroidery outlining as well as in-filling. The basic chain stitch can be worked double; the links can be extended sideways ('heavy chain stitch'); they can be knotted ('knotted chain stitch' or 'link stitch'); they can be opened into a square format ('open chain stitch', also known as 'square chain stitch' or 'ladder stitch'); they can be twisted, worked in zigzag shaping (known as 'zigzag chain stitch' or 'Vandyke chain stitch'); or individual links can be worked separately (known sometimes as 'daisy stitch').

Coral stitch, known variously as 'beaded stitch', 'coral knot', 'German knot stitch', 'knotted stitch' or 'snail's trail', is a useful 'linked thread' stitch. Each stitch forms a new knot in the chain. The stitch is generally worked fairly tightly to produce a neat trailing stitch.

88

Back stitch

Braid stitch

Buttonhole (blanket) stitch

Chain stitch

Coral stitch

Double-runing stitch

Herringbone stitch

Pekinese stitch

Speckling stich

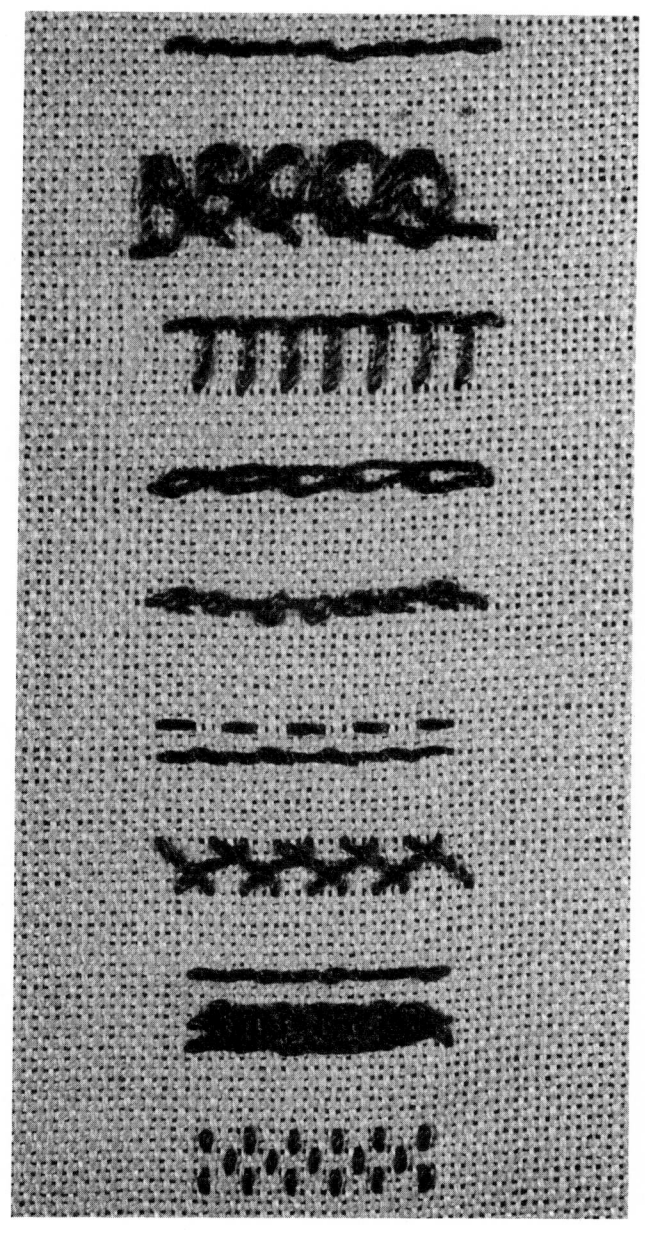

49 Some of the main stitches of 'historical' blackwork are (from the top) back stitch, braid stitch, buttonhole (blanket) stitch, chain stitch, coral stitch, double-running (Holbein) stitch, herringbone stitch, Pekinese stitch and speckling. Figure 49a shows drawings of the finished stitches. Figure 49b shows a photograph of the finished stitches. Figure 49c illustrates methods of working each stitch (see text)

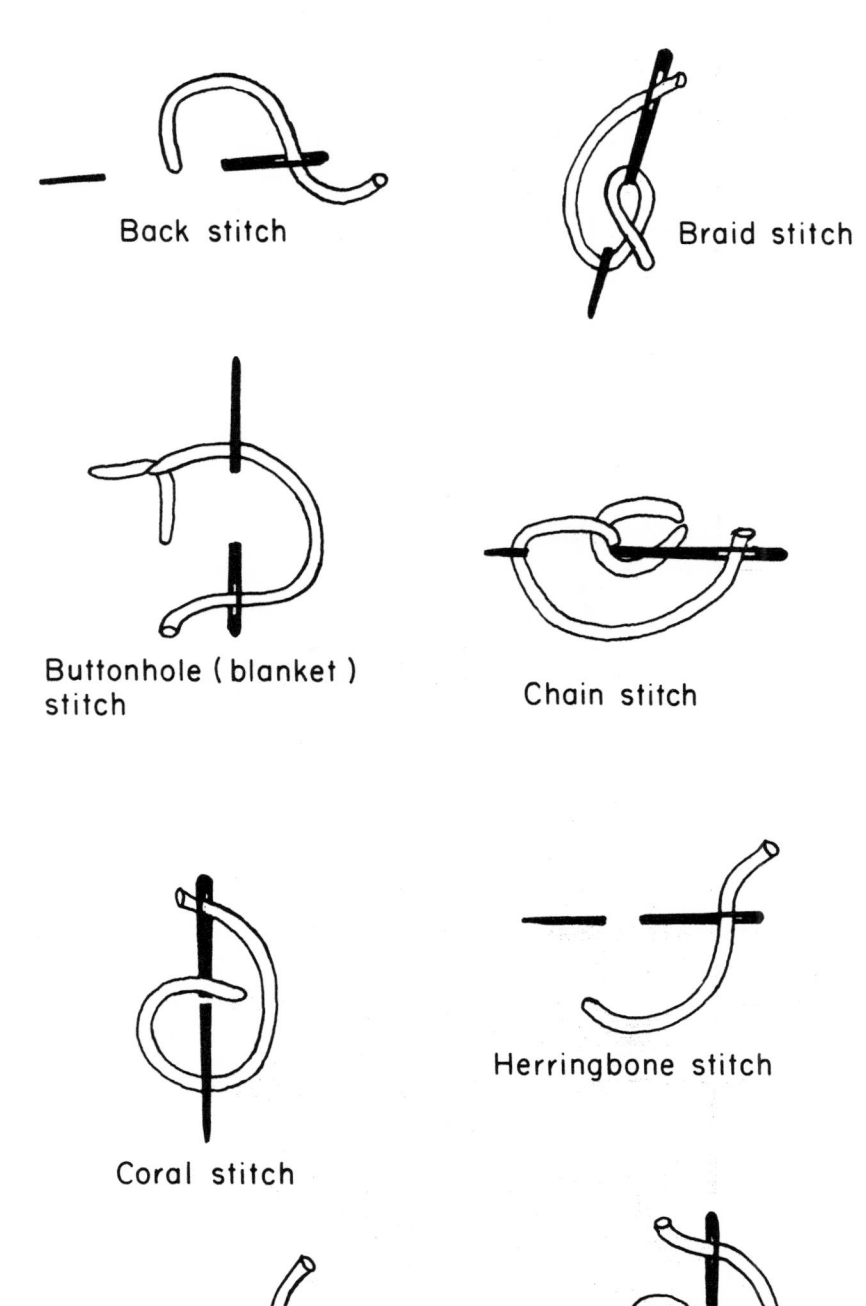

Back stitch

Braid stitch

Buttonhole (blanket) stitch

Chain stitch

Coral stitch

Herringbone stitch

Pekinese stitch

Double-running stitch is known also as 'Holbein stitch' because of the maestro's famous association with blackwork detailing. Other sobriquets for this stitch include 'line stitch', 'stroke stitch', 'square stitch', 'two-sided line stitch' and 'two-sided stroke stitch'. It has also been known as 'Romanian stitch' but this guise is not of immediate concern to blackwork embroiderers. Double-running stitch gives a finished appearance similar to that of back stitch. But whereas in back stitch each stitch is completed before the next is started, in double-running stitch the interstices formed by one line of running—or darning—stitch are themselves filled in during the second line of working. It is important, when working the second line of double-running stitch, to remember to bring the needle in and out of *the same side* of the stitches of the previous line. This will help give an even finished 'double line' of double-running stitch.

Herringbone stitch—why should the fish of this *Clupeidae* family have given its name to this crossed stitch which could, surely, be called after the backbone of so many fishes? The bones of the herring family have, since time immemorial, given their name to many crossed structures in forms of art other than embroidery: carpenters, to take one other example, refer to 'herringbone strutting' for crossed struts between floor joists. Herringbone stitch is also known as 'Indian filling', 'mossoul stitch', 'Russian stitch' and 'Russian cross stitch'. It is generally worked from left to right along an imaginary double line with each stitch crossing over its predecessor. The finished appearance of the stitching depends on the vertical and horizontal proportions of each individual stitch. A finished line of herringbone stitching can be subsequently interlaced for more dramatic effect.

Pekinese stitch or 'Chinese stitch' is thus called because of its frequent appearance in Chinese embroideries. The artists of Peking were particularly skilled in the past: they, the talented embroiderers of 'the Forbidden City', promulgated the use of the Peking (or Chinese) knot as a filling stitch, and eventually the knot itself was to be known occasionally as 'the Forbidden knot'. Pekinese stitch is formed over a line of back stitch. A second line of thread is worked in loops through each link of the back stitch: the second line of thread *does not enter the ground fabric at all*. It is a superficial line of threaded work.

Speckling or 'seeding' can also be known as 'dot stitch'. Tiny straight stitches, worked either at any angle or in geometric formation, provide a most effective filling.

Filling stitches play a most important role in blackwork embroidery. After the outline is worked—in chain stitch, back stitch, double-running or a similar stitch—the *in-filling* contributes to a great extent to the eventual density and appearance of a device. Other filling stitches used most effectively by historical blackwork embroiderers included rows of darning stitch (long straight running stitches), known sometimes as 'pessante', and vertical and horizontal lines of thread 'laid' over the surface of the ground fabric and the junctions held with small retaining stitches. The boxes formed by this 'trellis' could themselves be worked with another filling stitch.

The variety of filling stitches is really a personal challenge for the embroiderer. Old embroidery books frequently reveal 'new' stitches that must, surely, have been invented by the author herself. Some of the stitches included in the delightful book by M. E. Wilkinson (*Embroidery Stitches,* Herbert Jenkins, 1912) are a social commentary on the period. There is 'branching stitch', small straight stitches forming foliage 'used in the representation of branchings in natural needlework'. There is 'cricket stitch', a filling stitch formed by straight stitches worked like cricket stumps, with five horizontal stitches capped with one vertical stitch. And there is 'dumb-bell stitch', with lines of vertical straight stitches flanked by individual links of chain stitch (daisy stitch). What imagination author Wilkinson had when inventing some of these stitches!

The embroiderer of today can be similarly inventive, not only with names of stitches but also with combinations of basic embroidery stitches to provide complex patterning as required.

SAMPLERS

The novice blackwork embroiderer will probably want to experiment with stitches and will possibly want to work a sampler.

The word 'sampler' literally means a test piece, its name derived from the Latin *examplum* ('a pattern') via the French *essemplaire* and the Old English *ensample*. In the past most blackwork samplers have been worked in geometric formation on rectangular or square pieces of evenweave ground fabric.

This was the format followed by Mrs Boake who worked a superb blackwork sampler (figure 50) now in the collection of the Embroiderers' Guild. It represents an entire pattern book of different blackwork designs, most of them purely geometric but with a few humorous devices like the pair of snails, twentieth-century descendents of the animals so beloved of blackwork embroiderers nearly four hundred years before.

Sampler embroidery need not necessarily be a tedious exercise of copying stitch patternings. Peggy Ballard, an English embroiderer who is a prolific blackwork artist, produces exquisite needlecases and cushions, each one a sampler of geometric design, proof that sample working can be productive. Similar practical use was employed by Cynthia Stamp when she worked a blackwork sampler for her Diploma Course at the Royal School of Needlework in 1950. She worked her sampler on a hexagonal piece of linen, 30.5 cm × 34.3 cm (12 in × 13½ in), and composed a beautifully balanced 'picture', with an outer scroll bordering a design of buds and leaves. Each of the six segments is worked alternately in two combinations of different filling combinations, the stitches adapted from various older samplers at the Royal School. Some of the designs were taken from a 'redwork' sampler that possibly came from eastern Europe. The hexagonal pattern was worked in stranded cotton, perivale silk and ordinary sewing cotton with some highlight of gold twist.

When is a sampler not a sampler? Loreen Scheepers of Grahamstown, South Africa, worked her sampler (figure 51) in so pictorial a form that it is indeed a delightful 'finished product'. It is worked on white evenweave linen with thread count of 35 per 5 cm (14 per inch). The outline of the design is worked in No. 8 cotton, the filling in No. 12 cotton thread.

Loreen Scheepers worked her blackwork picture in a design not only associated with her own country but, also, with blackwork of all time. It is interesting to pair the Scheepers panel with a late sixteenth-century pillow cover (figure 52), embroidered with black silk in back stitch, chain stitch, cord stitch, braid stitch and

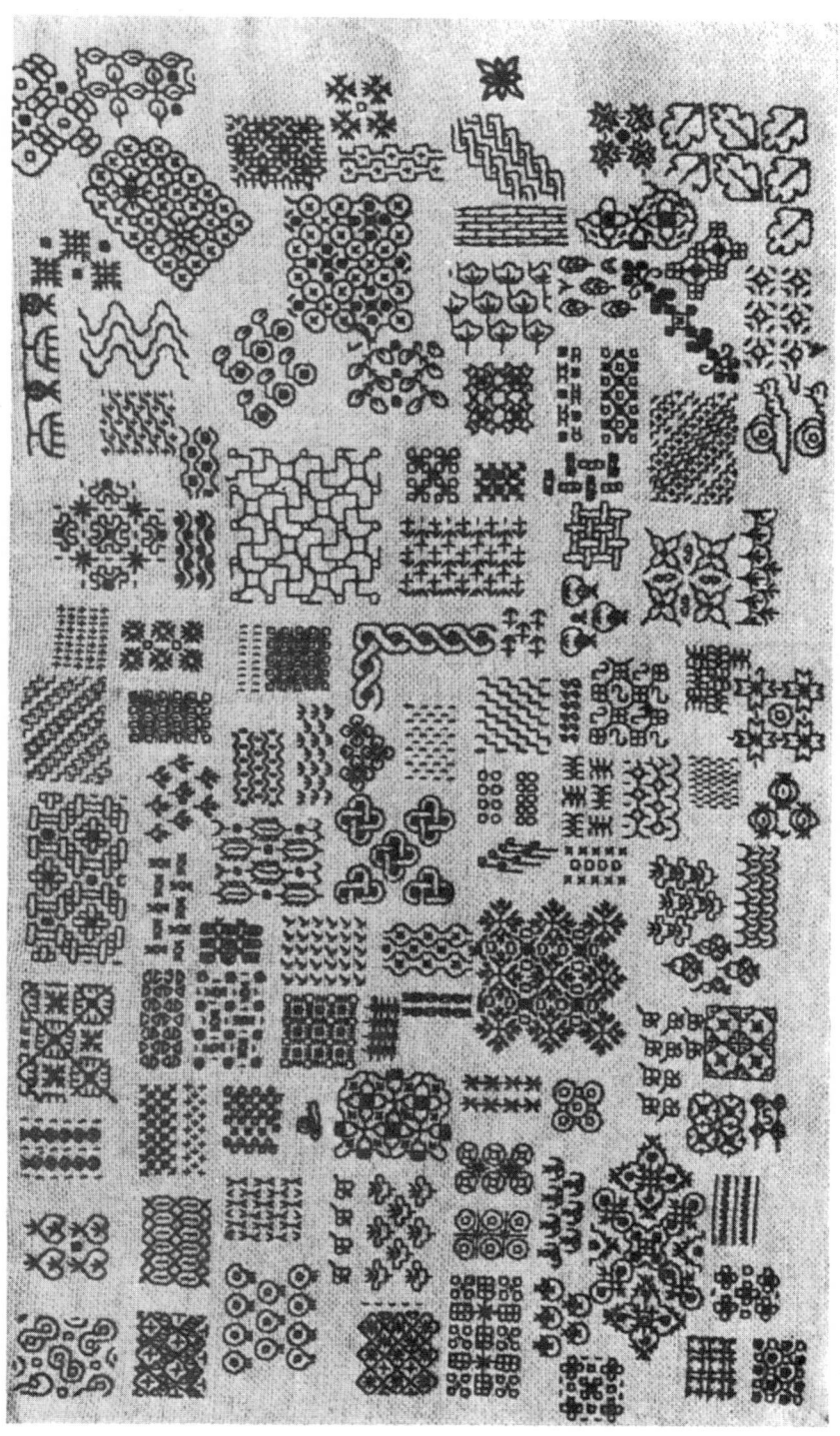

50 Sampler, 33 cm × 21 cm (13 in × 8¼ in), showing some of the most popular filling patterns, found in blackwork embroidery. (Embroiderers' Guild, No. 924)

51 Grape pattern worked by Loreen
Scheepers of Grahamstown, South Africa,
on a white evenweave linen ground 42
cm × 36 cm (16½ in × 14 in). *(Loreen
Scheepers)*

buttonhole stitch. Vine leaves and grapes have so often been employed by artists to symbolize the good life. And blackwork embroiderers have certainly contributed to this design form.

Sampler technique has sometimes been extremely skilfully executed in the form of 'cartographical blackwork'.

Enid Clinch, an English lady now living in South Carolina, worked a map of America to look like a 'printwork' embroidery. Her sampler (figure 53) is embroidered throughout in one strand of stranded cotton with the state borders outlined in coton perlé No. 8. Those states below the Mason–Dixon line are bordered in gold thread. The State of South Carolina is entirely worked in gold thread: Mrs Clinch finished her sampler in 1970, the tercentenary of the founding of that state.

Another map sampler (figure 54) was worked by Nancy Maxwell of Petone, New Zealand. Her embroidery is on a ground fabric of Swedish linen with a thread count of 72 per 5 cm (36 per inch). The outline of both the North and South Island is worked in coton à broder in back stitch. All the in-filling is worked in perivale silk.

Map samplers really do strengthen the association of blackwork embroidery with 'prints', 'engravings' and 'etchings', and it has already been suggested that in the past many outstanding examples of blackwork embroidery bore resemblance to other contemporary decorative art forms. Another association of blackwork embroidery is the similarity it bears to ordinary newsprint—a resemblance that can certainly be utilized when a design is conceived. . . .

96

52 Late sixteenth-century grape pattern,
worked on a pillow cover. *(Victoria and
Albert Museum, Crown Copyright, No.
T.81–1924)*

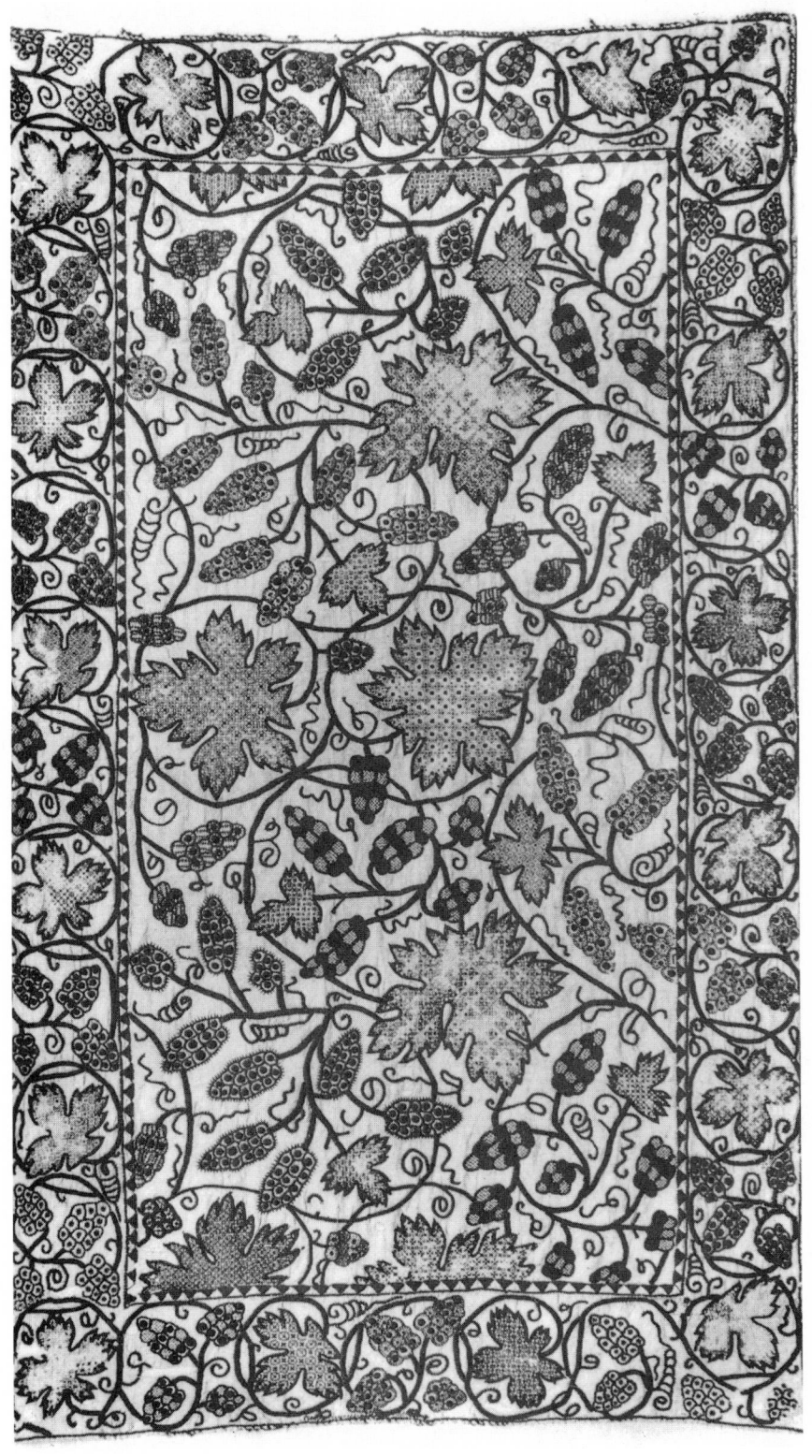

53 Map sampler worked by Enid Clinch of South Carolina. The sampler is 44.5 cm × 60.9 cm (17½ in × 24 in). The states below the Mason—Dixon line are bordered—and Mrs Clinch's own home state is worked throughout—in gold thread. *(Enid Clinch)*

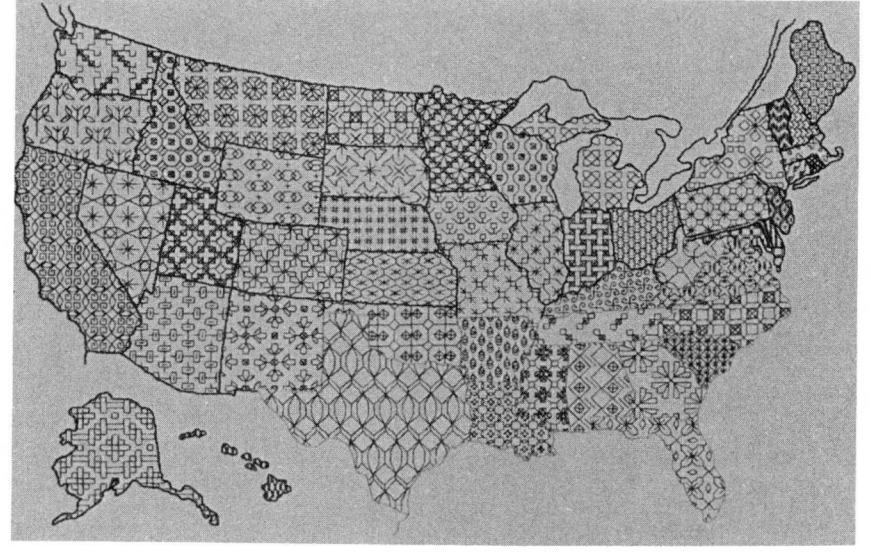

54 New Zealand map sampler, embroidered by Nancy Maxwell of Petone on a linen ground 71 cm × 40.6 cm (28 in × 16 in). *(Nancy Maxwell)*

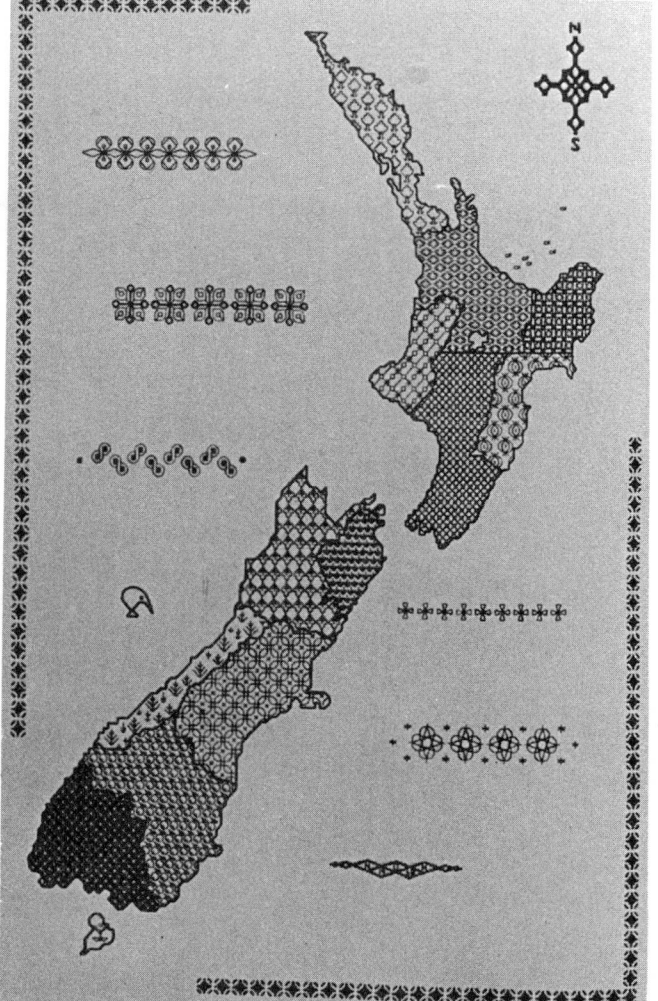

7 Designing Blackwork

One of the easiest methods of 'trying out' a desgn for density—and therefore for eventual effect—of blackwork is to use ordinary newsprint.

A newspaper is printed with assorted density of 'blackwork' printing that makes it ideal for embroidery pattern experimentation. Much of the print is black 'pointillism', with minute dots of black ink forming the overall pattern.

A single issue of *The Sunday Times* shows how a newspaper can be used to envisage a blackwork pattern. Particles were cut from various pages of the newspaper to produce a paper collage which was, in turn, reproduced in blackwork embroidery (figure 55). The density of newspaper printing will in many instances in fact exaggerate the eventual density—effect—of the finished blackwork embroidery. But this method of pattern conception is undoubtedly one of the easiest and most reliable ways of experimenting with different combinations of density for embroidery.

Another experimental transposition of design for blackwork was executed by Margaret Austin in a sampler of fruits and leaves. From initial drawings (figure 56a) taken from life, she prepared a basic pattern which she then worked (figure 56b) in geometric blackwork stitching experimenting with weight of thread and simplification of stitching. On a main ground, with a thread count of 40 per 5 cm (20 per inch), she worked a design of kowham, karamu and raraki. When looking at some of the filling stitches used in the Austin sampler, the effect of building up (or, in the reverse process, of simplifying) patterns becomes evident.

This progression of geometric design is an important element when envisaging use of filling stitches. Not only can the width of thread be varied to produce shading in one segment. But, either as an alternative or in addition, a pattern can itself be built up or cut down.

55 Pattern transposition. A simple clover design is 'sampled' in various shades of newsprint. The design is then worked on evenweave linen

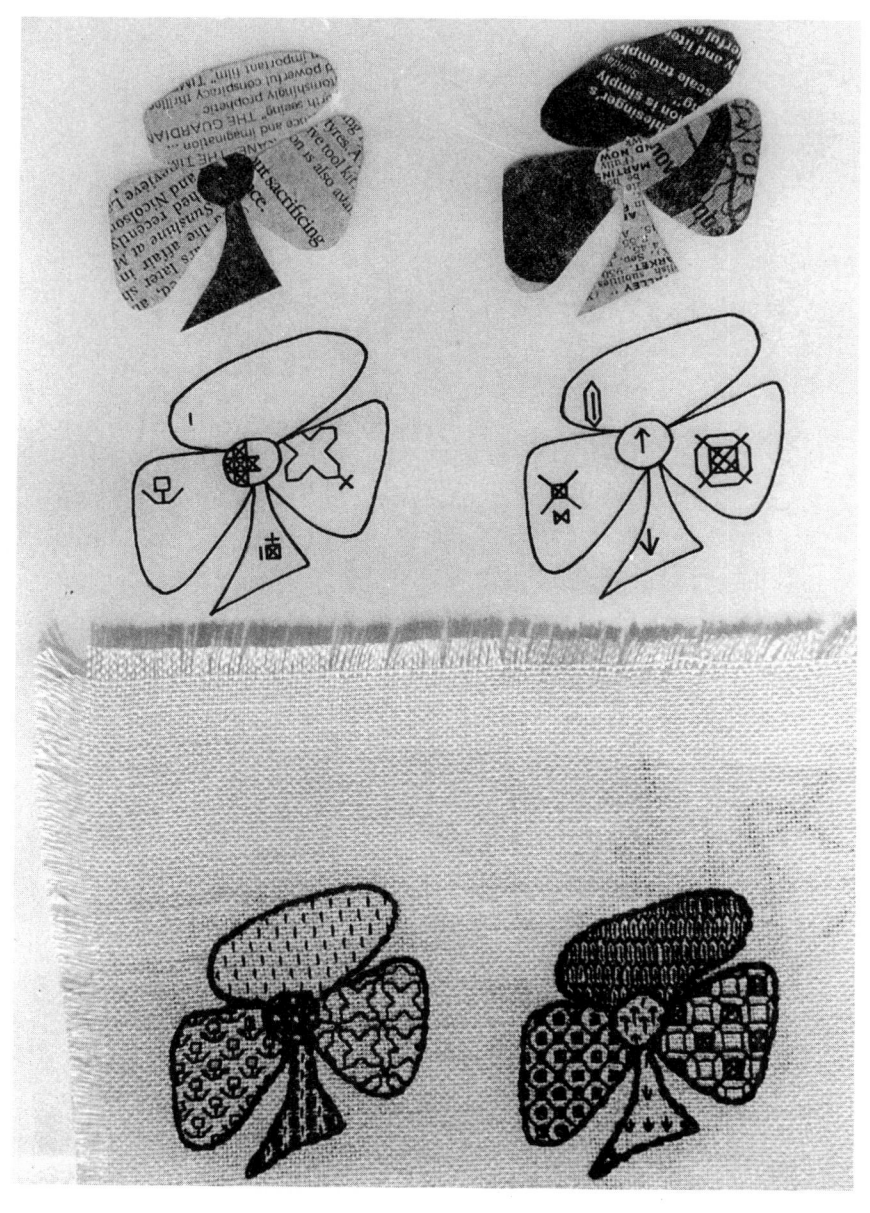

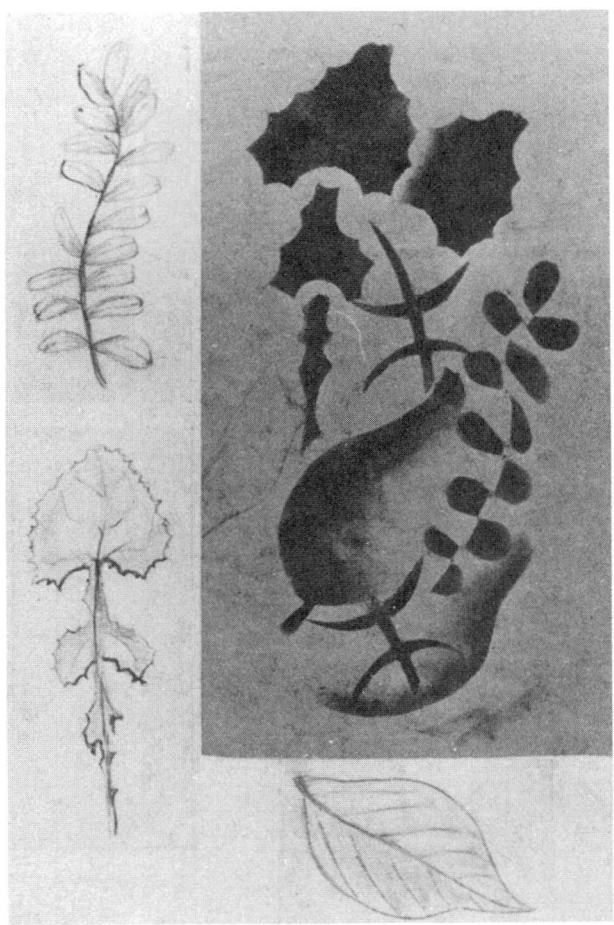 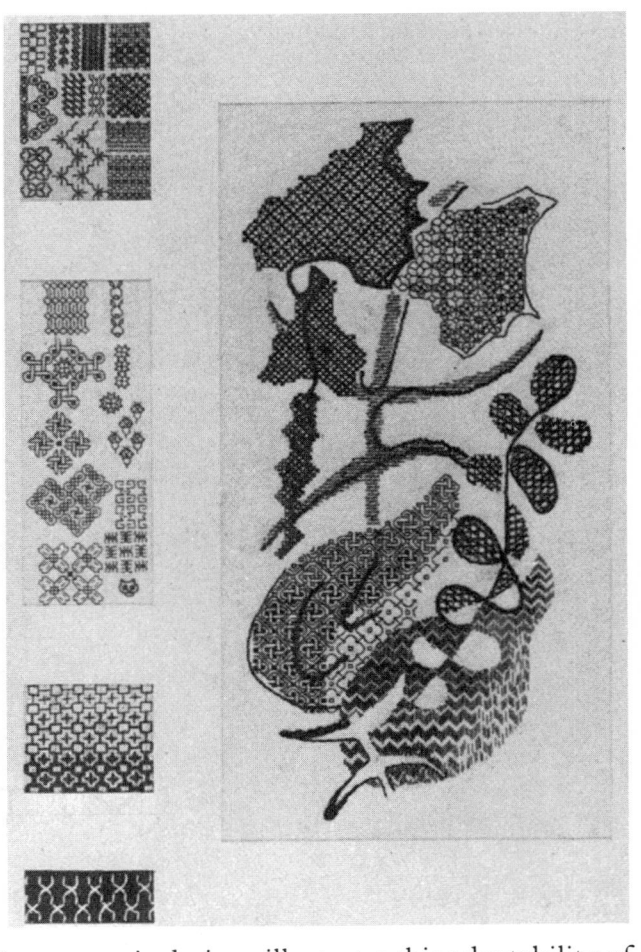

56 Margaret Austin's 36.2 cm × 18.4 cm
(14¼ in × 7¼ in) sampler (figure 56b) evolved
from sketches of fruit and leaves (figure
56a). She worked additional test patches of
filling stitches picture *(Margaret Austin)*

A quartet of basic geometric designs illustrates this adaptability of pattern. Mary Kay Sampson started with four simple geometric forms and built each up to a more complex pattern (figure 57). The more basic the original geometric shape, the more adaptable it will prove to be.

Some of these shapes are like old friends. The same box outlines and arrows, the same stars and crosses, patterns that have been used by embroiderers throughout the ages are skilfully employed by artists of today.

Helen M. Healy, a member of the Manawatu Embroiderers' Guild of New Zealand, incorporated many traditional 'blackwork patterns' in a panel (figure 58). A central rectangular interlaced border is itself surrounded by 'rays' of different geometric techniques. Density is carefully controlled so that the three most heavy rays of patterning balance the entire panel. Overall balance is thus aided by density of colour blocks and, also, by the length of the rays. Although balance is not so important in a plain working

57 Four 'progressive patterns' showing density variation achieved by additional working. These designs were taken from a sampler worked by Mary Kay Sampson.

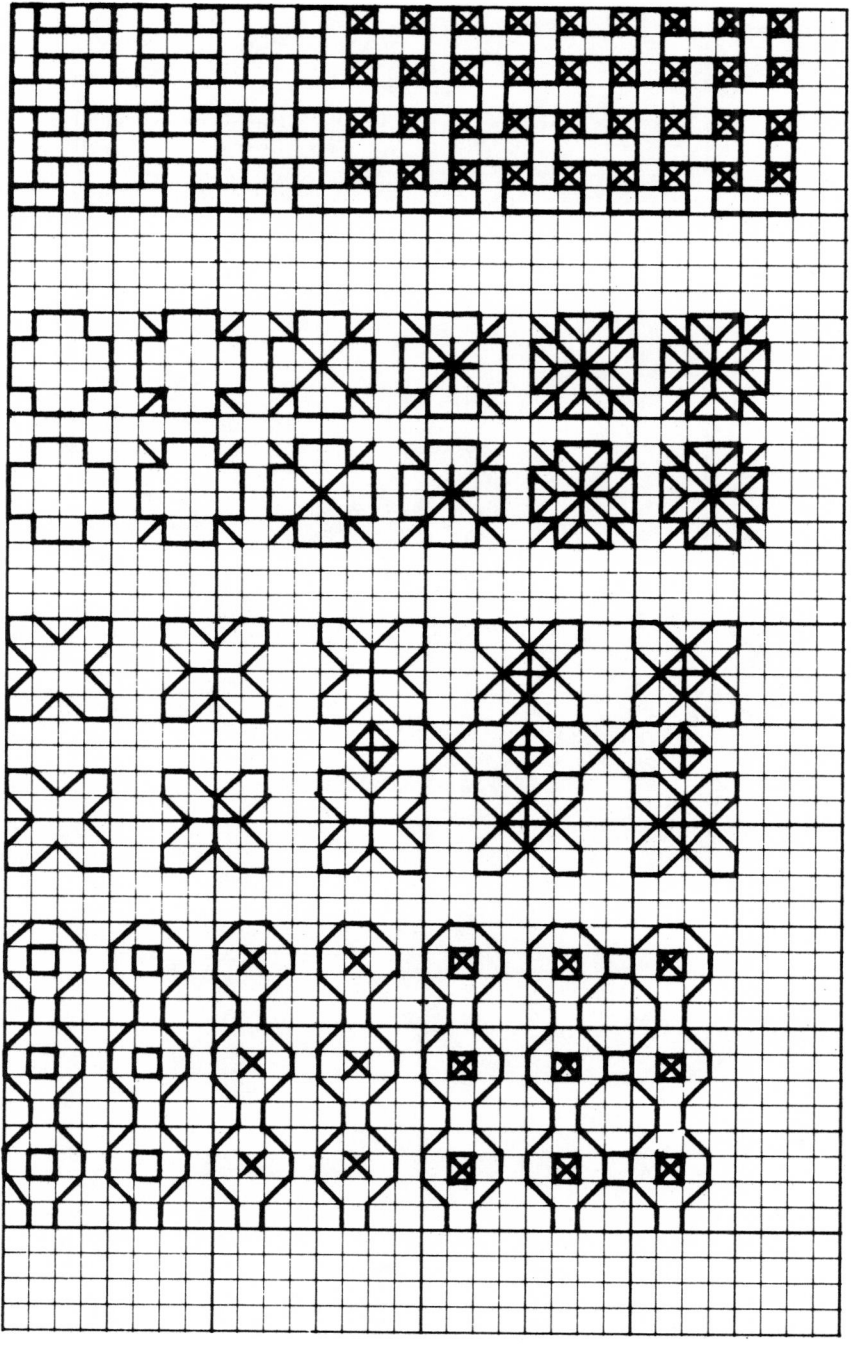

sampler, it is a vital element in the final effect of a blackwork picture or similar item, especially one intended for display or regular use. Balance can, in a really *pictorial* blackwork embroidery, constitute a major part of the importance of a work. A marvellous full-sailed galleon, designed by Helen Boswell in the studio of Vivienne Bam in Pretoria, was worked by the artist with such skilful use of density that it looks as if the vessel *is* having a difficult time in sailing against the wind. The heaviest blocks of colouring are reserved for the hull of the galleon and the two most aft sails.

58 Blackwork panel 35.6 cm (14 in) square, worked by Helen M. Healy of Manawatu. *(Helen M. Healy)*

Having studied the importance of density and balance of design, it is time to turn to the designs themselves. Whence can inspiration be gleaned?

To start with a simple theme, that of 'lots of boxes', step pattern formations can be copied from some most surprising sources.

A printed fabric used for men's shirts designed and sold in Lebanon gives inspiration to the imaginative embroiderer (figure 59). The original outline step form looks as if each device is identical but this is in fact an optical illusion. There are two different variants of the pattern, spaced alternately over the ground. The step outline can be built up in many different ways.

Other step patterns have been charted by M. Jacques Revault, a Tunisian art historian with a special interest in ethnographical textile design from all countries of northern Africa. Many of his carpet and printed textile shapes transpose ideally to blackwork embroidery. To follow the 'lots of boxes theme', M. Revault includes in his folio of *Tapis tunisiens* (now republished as *Designs and Patterns from North African Carpets and Textiles*, Dover Publications, 1973) three step-box patterns from Gafsa, or Capsa, an oasis in southern Tunisia which has long been famous for its blanket designs. The three Gafsa designs (figure 60) included in this box anthology are called 'spiders' webs', 'webs with tents' and 'superimposed webs'. The superimposition of the last 'web' can be studied in relation to another step pattern, one that is reversed rather than superimposed the one on the other, in the same selection of 'lots of boxes'.

Edward B. Edwards (1873–1948) was an American designer and illustrator who adapted many of the principles and designs of artists of ancient times. He stated: 'It is just as important for the designer to understand the laws of harmoniously related forms and areas as it is for the musical composer to be familiar with the laws of harmony and counterpoint.' Some of Edwards' designs, first published in *Dynamarhythmic Design* (1932), are directly reproducible as blackwork embroidery (figure 61). Alternating squares of gnomons of the 1.618 rectangle and of its reciprocal in different filling stitches would make a striking blackwork border. The box appearance of these border ideas bears relation to the geometric theme found in some early American hooked rug patterns. Once again, carpet textile designs can be transposed to blackwork embroidery: a three-dimensional pattern for a hooked rug (figure 62), as reproduced in *Descriptive Catalogue of E. S. Frost and Co.'s Hooked Rug Patterns* (Greenfield Village, 1970, No. 58), can well be adapted to different filling stitches for blackwork embroidery.

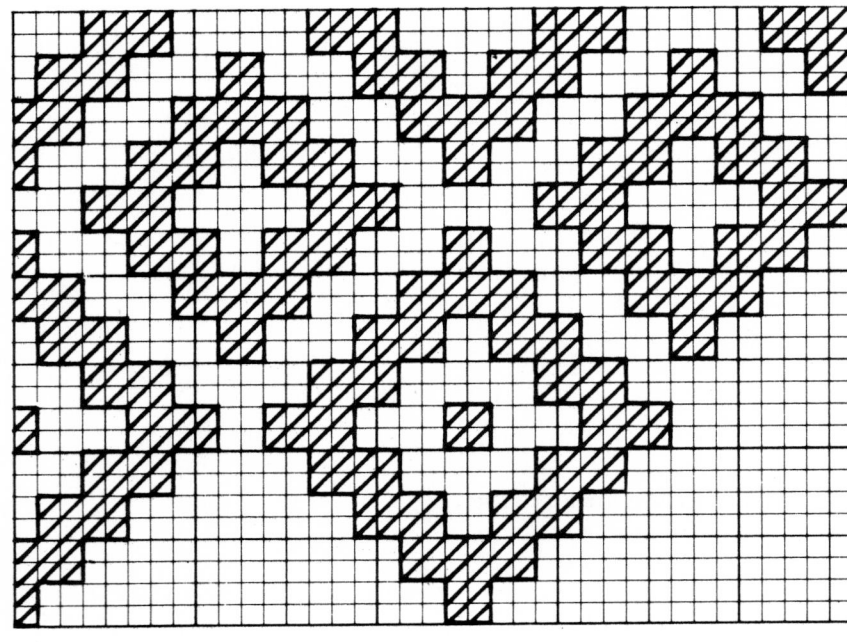

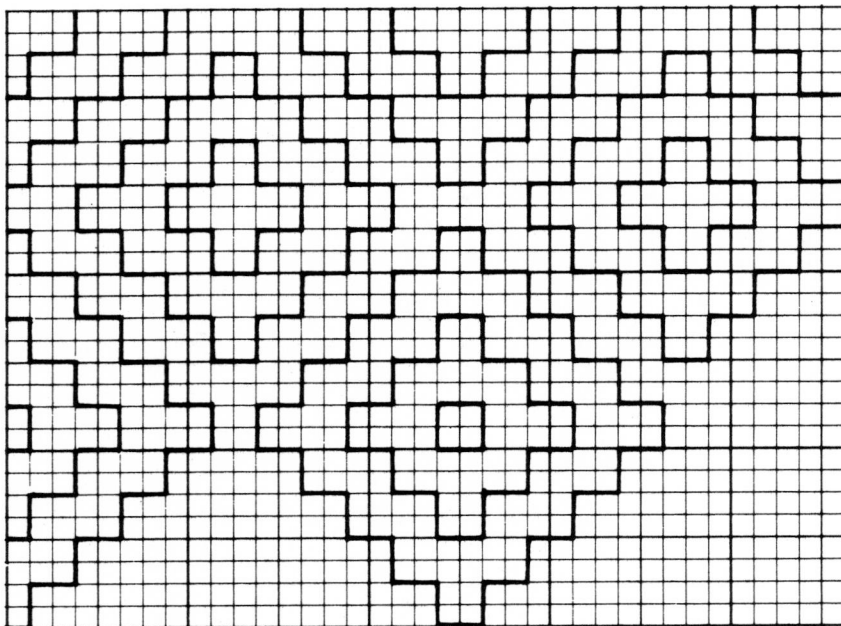

59 A simple step pattern taken from a
Lebanese man's shirt (figure 59a) can be
adapted to a variety of lots of boxes'
designs (figures 59 b, c). (Mr Sohel Fuad
Rached)

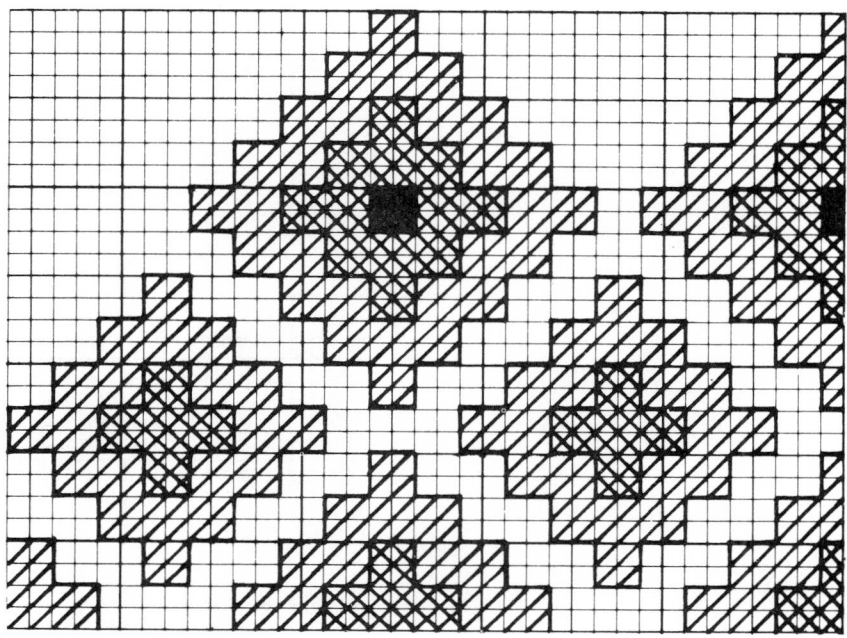

Another theme stressed by Edward Edwards is the Greek key or fret pattern, a basic art shape found in all parts of the world. The designs (figure 63) included in the sequence of key patterns are here taken from a pre-Colombian Inca pattern from Peru, from Rhodes, from a traditional Chinese cross stitch pattern (reproduced by Antoinette Prip-Møller in *Cross Stitch Patterns*, Thelma M. Nye, 1969) and from an embroidery worked in homespun wool on evenweave Indian cotton by Robin Jeffcoat of Wollongong, New South Wales.

Ethnographic designs can thus be gathered from all over the world. Marken is an island near Amsterdam renowned both for its tourist trade and for its polychrome wool embroideries. Some of the patterns found on those many-coloured embroideries can be adapted to blackwork, as illustrated wth two simple border panels (figure 64). A survey of indigenous design could include, too, devices worked by the 'leathermen' of Zaria City in Nigeria. These designs (figure 65) have been catalogued and identified by the art historian David Heathcote of Ahmadu Bello University, Zaria, and the three motifs shown here, all of which easily transpose to blackwork embroidery, are different interpretations of the interwoven knot, itself a theme that is found in ethnographic designs as far afield as Iceland, China and in many other countries.

As a contrast to the severity of some of these lines, the more graceful movement of the arabesque offers a welcome *divertissement*.

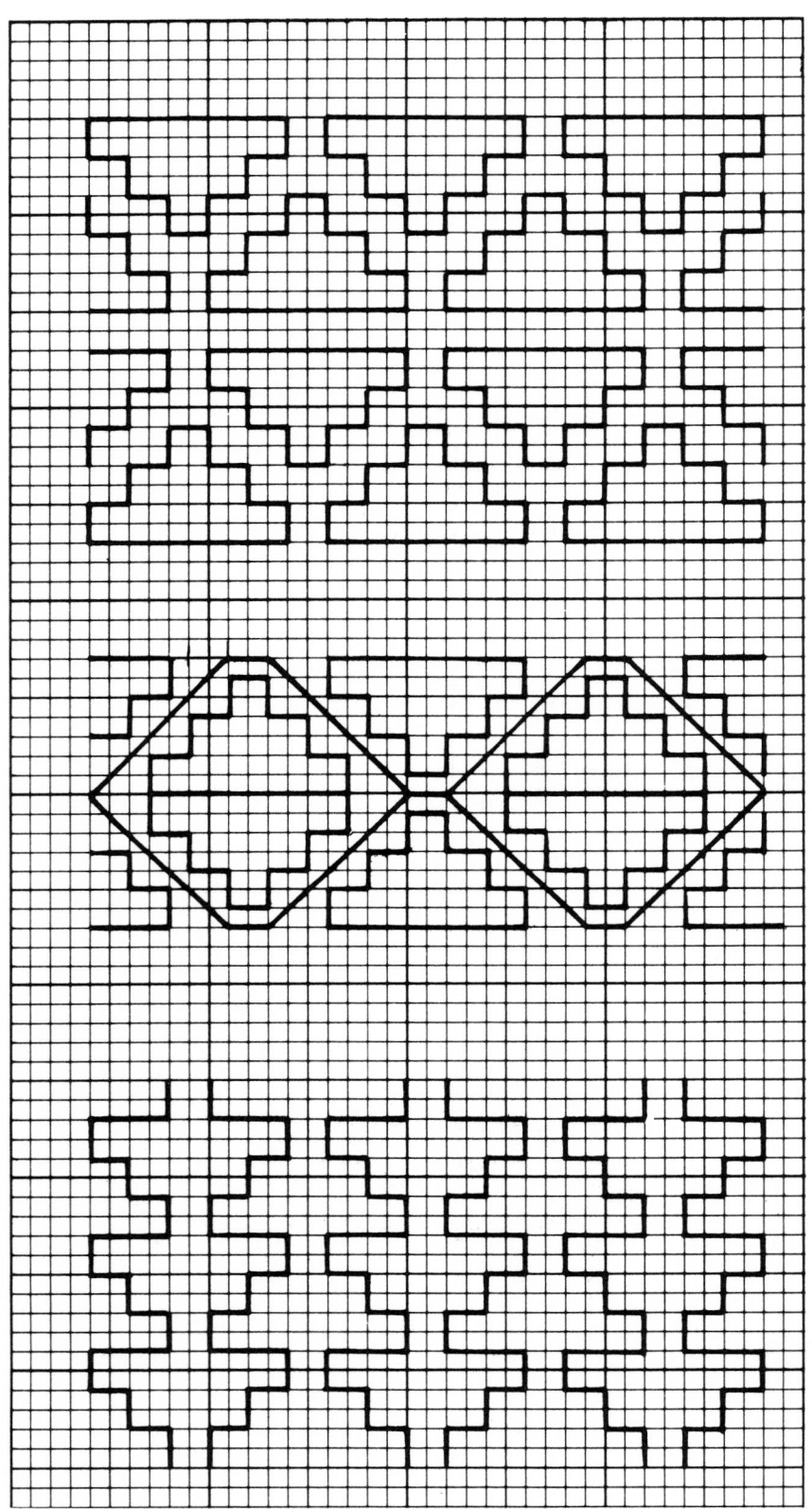

60 Three Gafsa carpet patterns from
southern Tunisia that can be adapted to
blackwork embroidery: a, 'spiders' webs'; b,
'webs with tents'; c, superimposed webs'.
(*Taken from Designs and Patterns from
North African Carpets and Textiles, Dover
Publications, 1973, by kind permission of
the publishers*)

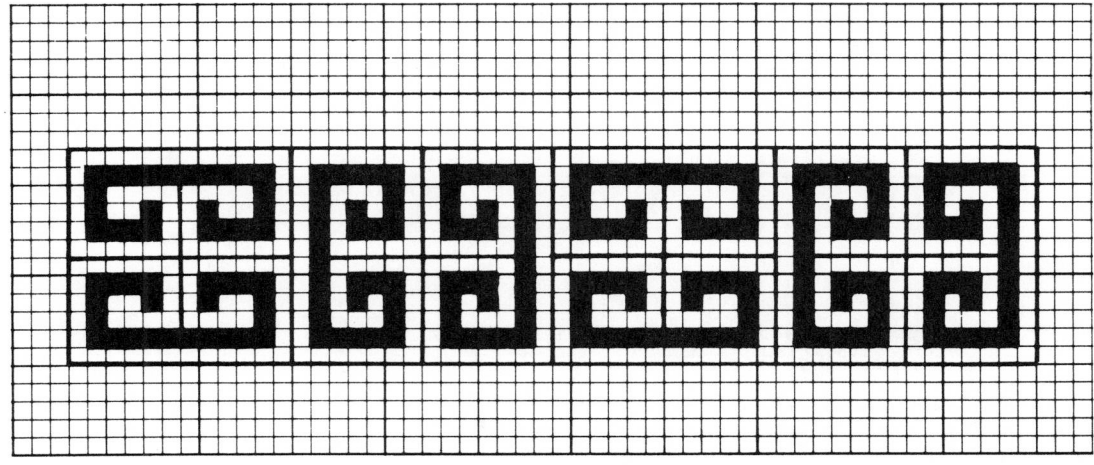

63 Key or fret patterns from many parts of the world : a, key design by Edward B. Edwards (reproduced by kind permission of Dover Publications)

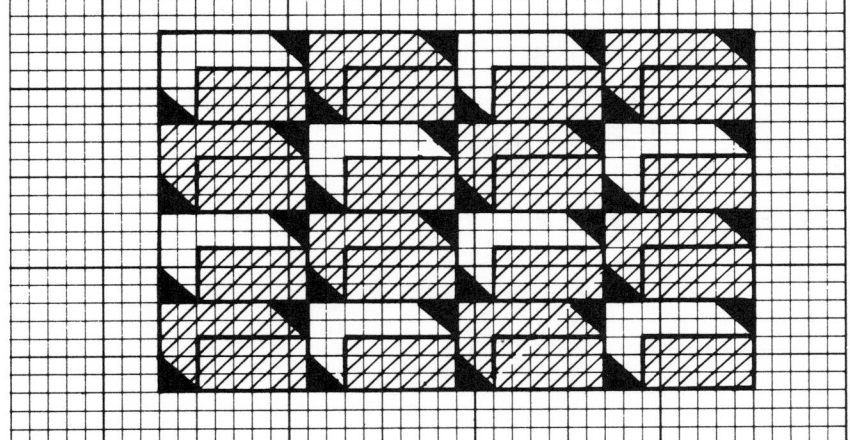

62 Another 'three-dimensional' pattern taken from a hooked rug design. (Collections of Greenfield Village and the Henry Ford Museum, Dearborn, Michigan)

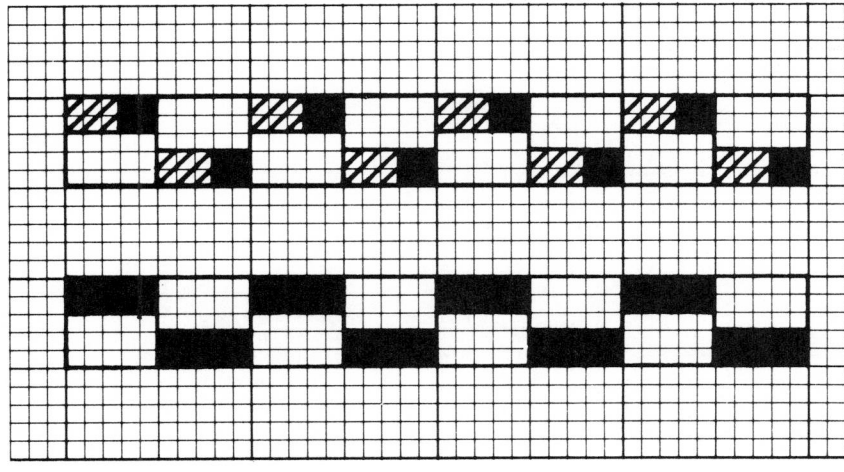

61 Two geometric designs by Edward B. Edwards (1873–1948), an American designer and illustrator. (Taken from Pattern and Design with Dynamic Symmetry, Dover Publications, 1967, by kind permission of the publishers)

108

b, design on a wool
embroidery by Robin Jeffcoat of
Wollongong, New South Wales; c. Italian
design, 8 B.C.; d, Peruvian design, pre-
Colombian Inca; e, Rhodes design; f, a
traditional Chinese cross stitch pattern (as
shown by Antoinette Prip-Møller. *Cross
Stitch Patterns*, ed. Thelma M. Nye,
Batsford, 1969)

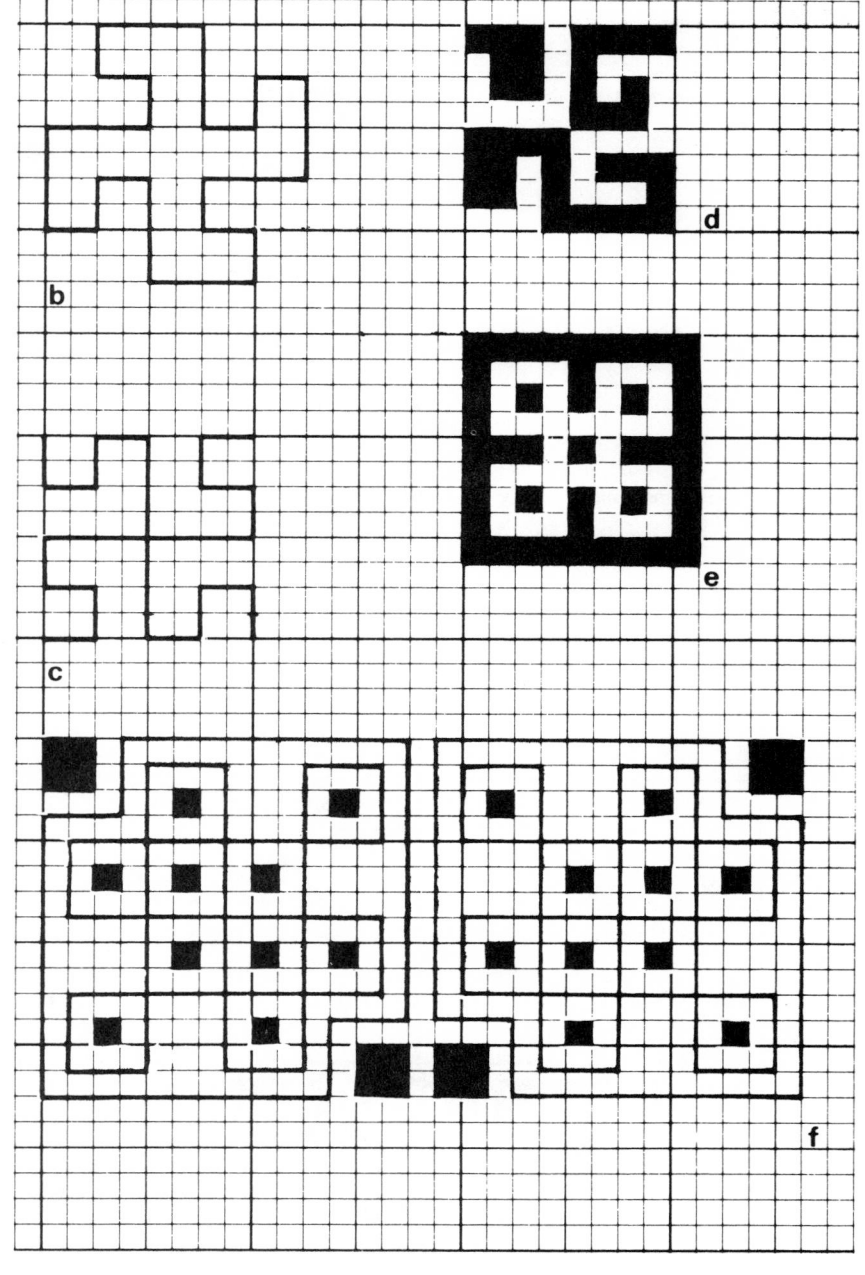

64 Ethnographic designs from Marken, the island near Amsterdam renowned for its tourists and for its polychrome wool embroideries. *(Reproduced by kind permission of Rijksmuseum voor Volkskunde, Arnhem, from Maria van Hemert,* De Handwerke of Hat Eiland Marken*)*

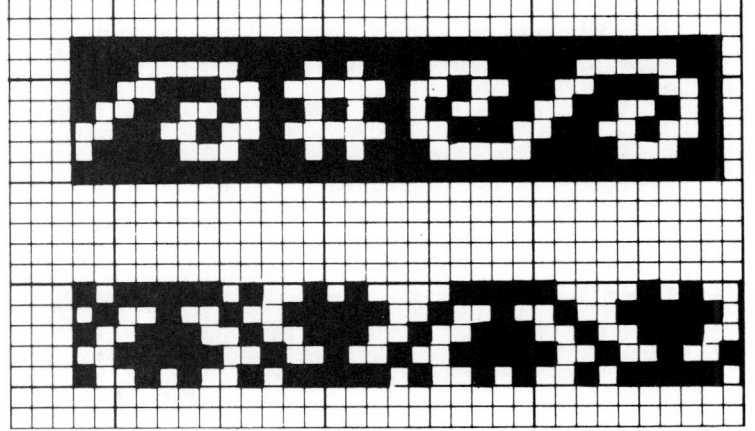

65 Three variations of diagonal patterns taken from designs used by leather workers in Zaria City, Nigeria. *(Mr David Heathcote)*

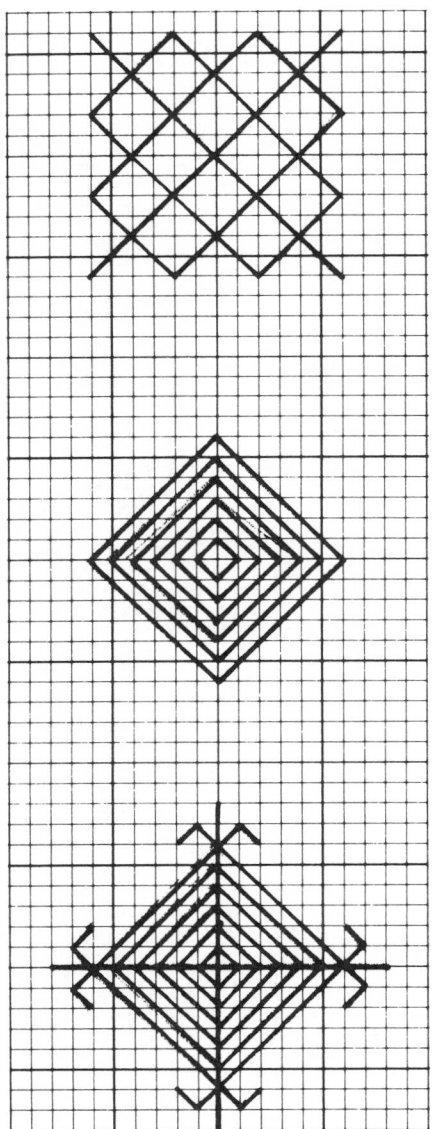

66 Arabesque for all occasions: a, candle shape taken from an embroidery by Ezanne Steward; b, circular arabesque sun taken from a cloth, 33 cm × 25 cm (13 in × 9¾ in), in the collection of the Embroiderers' Guild (No. 125); c, corner of an 'octagonal' arabesque on a late 19th century Russian tablecloth; d, corner design taken from a cloth in the collection of the Embroiderers' Guild (No. 1113)

Although blackwork embroidery must be controlled and exact it should at no time—either during execution or in effect when finished—be boring. Blackwork is *fun*.

Since the arabesque is itself synonymous with those early designs of the Moors, what more natural design exists to break up the ranks of right-angled geometric shapes? Various forms of the arabesque illustrate how it can be worked in counted-thread design. A candle-tree shape (figure 66a) is taken from an embroidery worked in 1975 by Ezanne Steward of New York City. A circular sun shape (figure 66b) is taken from an Italian cloth worked in double-running and cross stitch. A corner motif (figure 66c) is taken from the same collection. An octagonal arabesque (figure 66d) is adapted from a late nineteenth-century Russian towel in a private collection now in London. The original of this last design was executed in pink silk on a linen ground but it would transpose well to blackwork embroidery.

From the fluid movement of the arabesque to nature, ever a source of enjoyment to embroiderers. . . .

Betty Vanderbilt worked a fern picture (figure 67), 'Natural Grace', on a linen ground. The linen has a thread count of 58 per 5 cm (29 per inch) and it was originally worked in deep red silk monochrome embroidery with some highlighting of Jap gold. The same movement of design that is associated wth arabesque patterning is found in this picture. The curvilinear outlines are well balanced by the geometric in-filling. It will be noticed that the top left-hand butterfly is filled with a progressive pattern.

One of the most popular design motifs favoured by embroiderers in many parts of the world is that of 'the tree of life'. It has often been suggested that the idea of the tree as textile decoration originated in the east but the appearance of such famous embroideries as the 'Coronation Mantle', that highly sophisticated cloak embroidered at the beginning of the twelfth century in Palermo, Sicily, for the Norman Kings, has already shown that the tree of life was present, in one of its many forms, in occidental embroidery.

The tree of life has stimulated much study of its symbolism. Blackwork embroiderers can gather ideas from studies of the various forms of tree like that written by Roger Cook (*The Tree of Life,* Thames and Hudson, 1974), a marvellous anthology that delves into the trees of imagination, fertility, ascent, sacrifice, knowledge, history, inner necessity, the tree at the centre and the inverted tree. For all its inner meanings, however, a basic structural tree of life nonetheless continues to inspire embroiderers to produce new variants of 'blackwork sampler'.

67 'Natural Grace', a design taken from
ferns. The embroidery, designed and worked
by Betty Vanderbilt, is 58.4 cm (23 in)
square and it is on evenweave linen with
thread count of 58 per 5 cm (29 per inch).
(Betty Vanderbilt)

68 'The Tree of Life', as developed by
Nancy Stolarsky on a panel 40.6 cm × 35.6
cm (16 in × 14 in). *(Nancy Stolarsky)*

69 A variation of 'The Tree', as worked by
Marsha Katzman on another 40.6 cm × 35.6
cm (16 in × 14 in) panel. *(Marsha Katzman)*

114

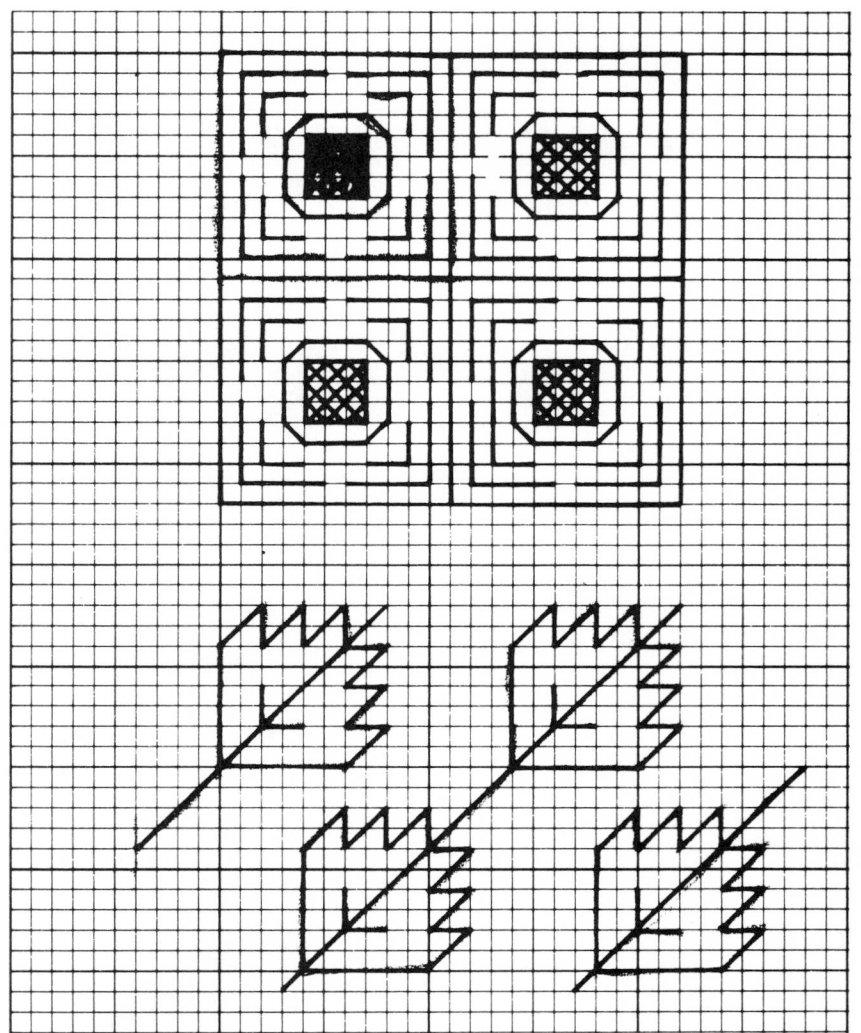

70 A flower garden of blackwork panels, with designs adapted from pieces worked by Heather Joynes and E. de la Rosa (to the design of Hetsie van Wyk.

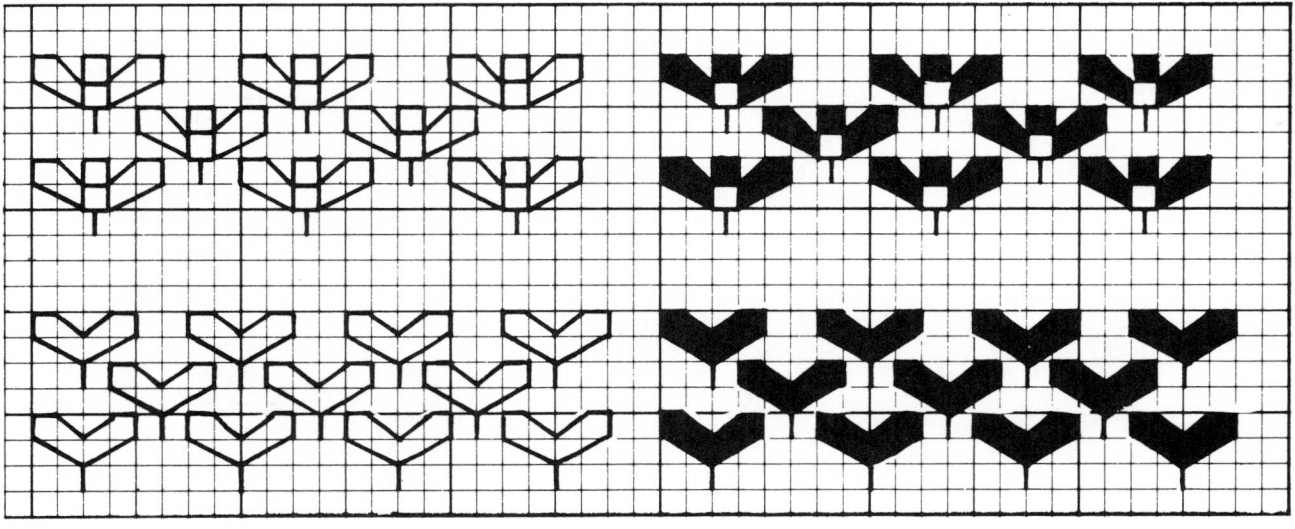

Two trees of life (figures 68 and 69), both rising from earthly mounds or 'terra firma', reiterate the effect that can be produced when geometric forms are contained in flowing outlines. Both trees were worked on evenweave linen with thread count of 36 per 5 cm (18 per inch) and both designs were executed in coton perlé No. 8. The overall design of each is 40.6 cm × 35.6 cm (16 in × 14 in) and the similarity of the trees is produced by the fact that they were both adapted from the same original pattern.

Both Marsha Katzman and Nancy Stolarsky have included in their many geometric filling patterns designs that are themselves particularly associated with floral symbolism. It is appropriate when, for instance, the mounds of earth at the foot of a tree of life are filled with grass or 'miniature tree' patterns as they are in both these illustrations. Floral devices are not without a chameleon-like quality and many of the most popular 'flower patterns' could be equally well interpreted as 'ladybirds' (or 'ladybugs'). But the suitability of matching filling devices to overall theme is an important element in prize-winning construction of blackwork embroidery.

A dip into a flower garden (figure 70) of filling shapes illuminates the variety of 'plants' available to the floral blackwork embroiderer. Some of the flower designs have been copied from those included in 'Garden Plan', a 17.2 cm ($6\frac{3}{4}$ in) square sampler worked by Heather Joynes. The design with thistle resemblance is from a cloth worked by E. de la Rosa to a pattern by Hetsie van Wyk. And other flowers are taken from various pieces in the collection of the Embroiderers' Guild (figure 70a).

The similarity of some blackwork 'flowers' to insects has already been noted. All forms of animal life have been recreated in blackwork—or other one-colour—embroidery. Birds exotic, imaginary and ordinary have been stitched by blackwork embroiders. Two very different bird themes (figure 71a, b) show the spectrum through which blackwork embroidery can pass, from the rather feathery appearance of a bird with full plumage, as seen on a late nineteenth-century towel from Russia now in a private collection in London, to a square counted-thread bird, part of a rectangular design that was set in 1930 by the Women's Institutes of Surrey and Warwickshire in an important embroidery competition. In both instances the birds themselves are merely part of the overall design.

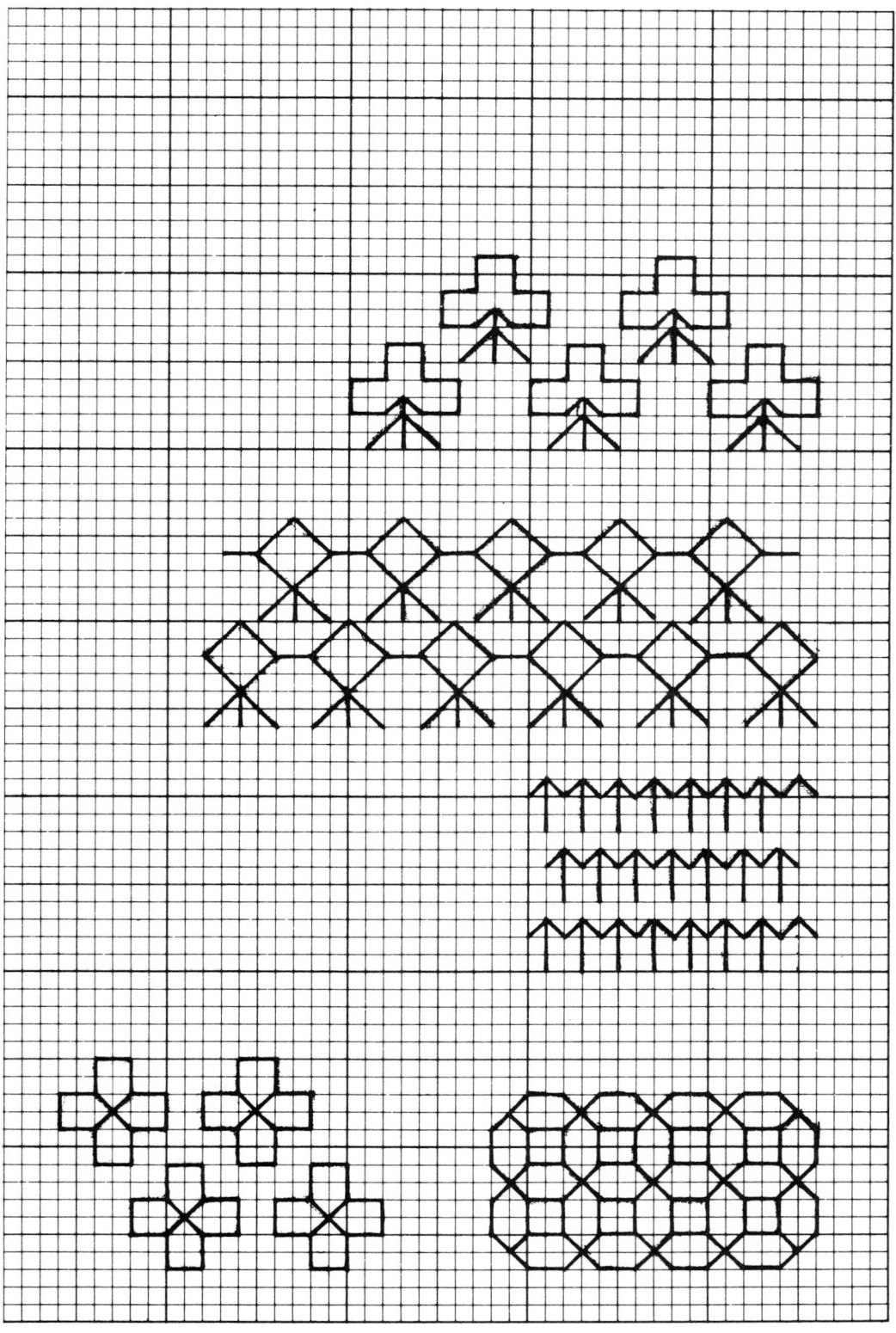

70a Flowers from material in the collection
of the Embroiderers' Guild.

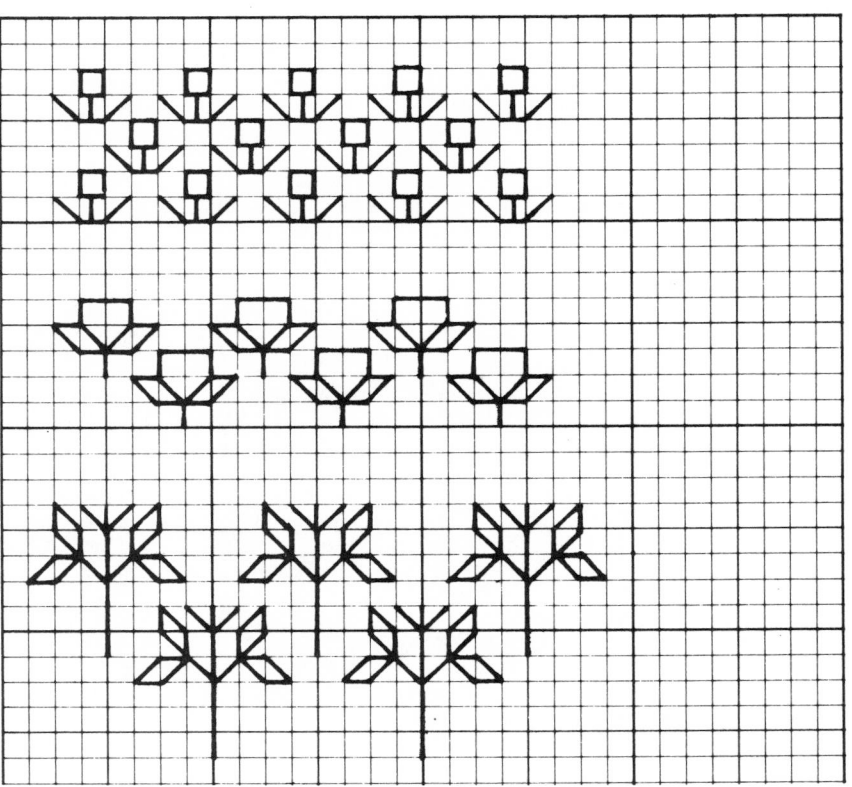

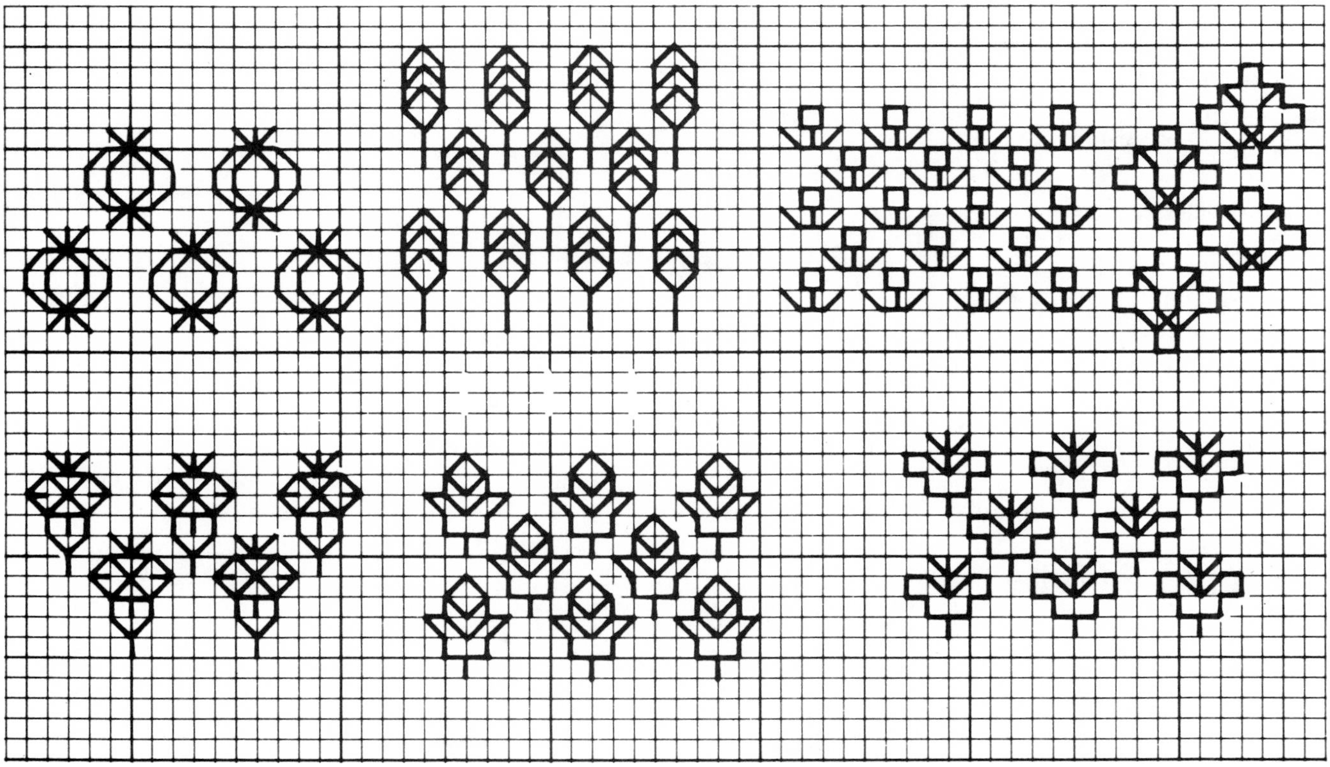

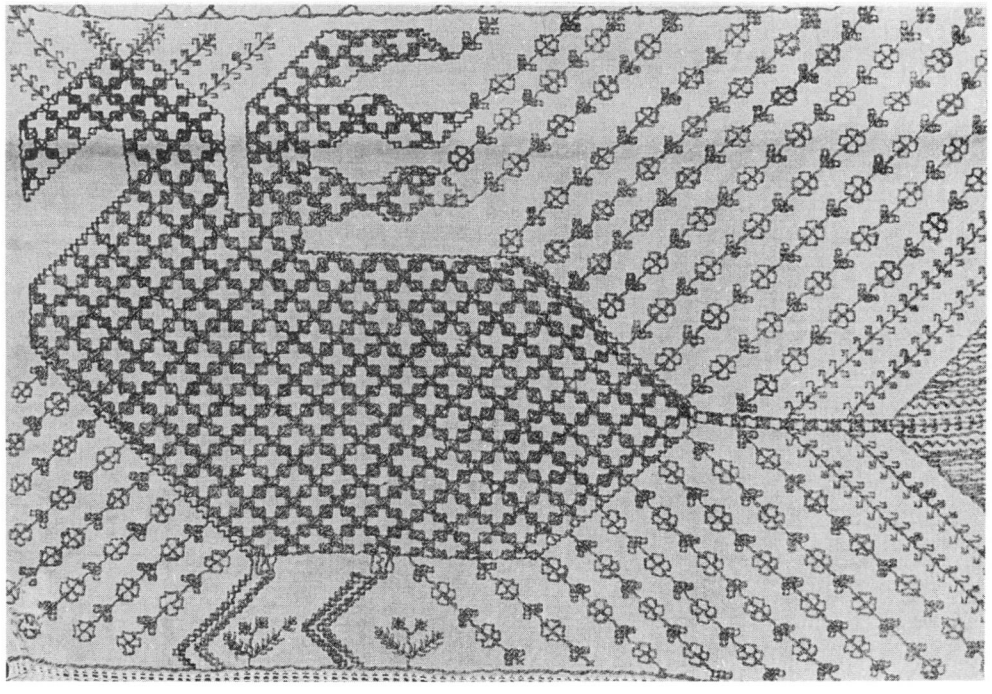

71 Bird patterns for blackwork: a, late nineteenth-century Russian bird on a tablecloth; b, design produced in 1930 as part of a competition set by the Women's Institutes of Surrey and Warwickshire.

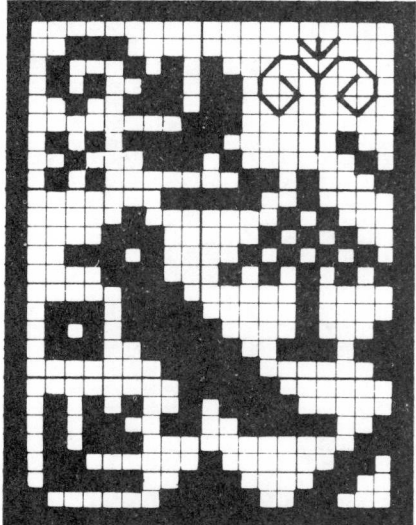

What happens to the keen blackwork embroiderer who does not feel confident of trying an original design? There are always old pieces of blackwork to copy. There are commercial kits and transfers available. And designs can be copied from many other facets of the decorative arts.

Maxine Ziemba of New York City copied her 'Lady with a Golden Fruit' (figure 72) from a greetings card. She worked her embroidery on evenweave linen with a thread count of 58 per 5 cm (29 per inch). The entire picture is glazed, and the embroidery is worked in 'mouliné spécial' with highlights in lurex.

Gillian Ridler went further back in time for her inspiration. She took the design (figure 73) for a blackwork figure of a lady kneeling at a prayer desk from a sixteenth-century brass of the same size. The brass, of Lady Monoux, is in St Mary's Church in Walthamstow and the Ridler embroidery is worked in geometric designs that recreate the density, and effect, of the original. One of the most interesting points about this embroidery is how parts of the ground fabric that are left plain, unworked, tend to highlight the ultimate design. Embroidery has much in common with other arts like painting, sculpture—even speech-making! The novice tends to fight shy of bare ground fabric, unworked canvas, wood—silences between sentences—or whatever the art form so constitutes. It takes courage and experience for an embroiderer thus to have 'command' of empty ground fabric.

72 A greetings card design transposed by
Maxine Ziemba on an evenweave linen
ground 43.2 cm × 29.2 cm (17 in × 11½ in).
(Maxine Ziemba)

73 Gillian Ridler's blackwork design came
from a brass of Lady Monoux in St Mary's
Church, Walthamstow. Her embroidery is
the same size—39.4 cm × 24.1 cm (15¼
in × 9½ in)—as the pattern. She has left Lady
Monoux's hands unworked. *(Gillian Ridler)*

74 Hands also play a focal role in Dorothy
B. Lang's 'The Faithful Eleven', 24.1
cm × 60.9 cm (9½ in × 24 in). *(Dorothy B.
Lang)*

The hands of the Ridler embroidery help, by their very simplicity,
to lend interest to the design. Jesus' hands similarly become one of
the focal points of 'The Faithful Eleven', a blackwork by (figure
74) Dorothy B. Lang of Boulder, Colorado. The recreation of the
Last Supper is worked in 24 different filling stitches. Only Our
Lord's hands are left unworked. His upright stance, the rays
coming from His head, and the solid blocking of the table around
which the disciples are gathered also bring the attention to the
centre of this picture.

Because of the confusion created by some smaller partitions in a
complex blackwork embroidery, it is necessary, when creating a
blackwork *picture* as opposed to a *sampler*, to give balance through
perspective or arrangement of sections of the design.

Looking at architectural drawings and photographs can inspire
blackwork embroiderers and, at the same time, help with perspective transposition. An historical map (figure 75) like 'A
Portraiture of the City of Philadelphia' could be a model to an
embroiderer. The map was produced 'In the Province of Pennsylvania in America by Thomas Holme, Surveyor General. Sold
by John Thornton in the Minories and Andrew Sowle in
Shoreditch, London, 1683'. It is the original plan of Philadelphia as
drawn by the surveyor to William Penn. Holme, a Quaker who had
once served with Cromwell's army in Ireland, first arrived in
Philadelphia in 1682 and he planned the city so that all the main
purchasers of the operative stocks of the Free Society of Traders
might have properties along the 'Fronts (and the High-street)'
whilst lesser stock-holders had to suffice with 'about half an Acre
in the backward Streets'. The original map was 29.2 cm × 43.8 cm

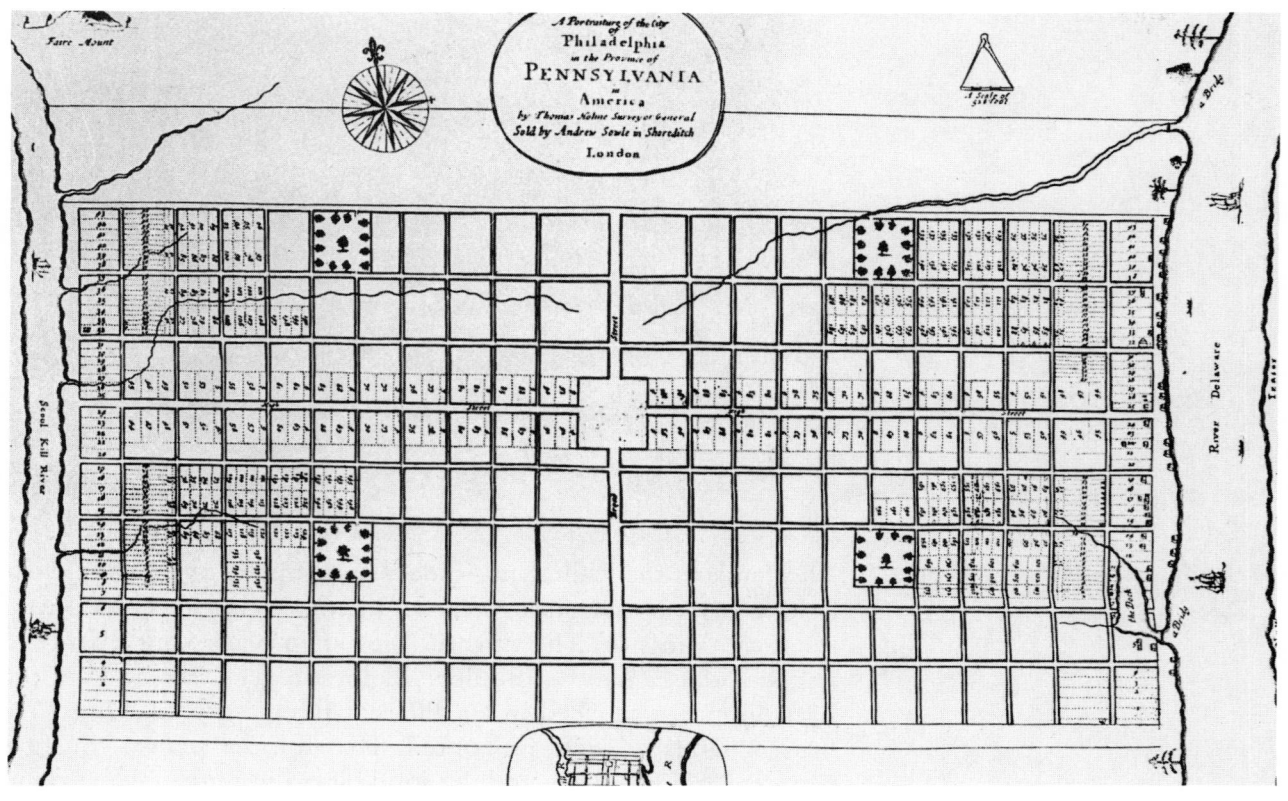

75 Inspiration from an old map. This, 'A
Portraiture of the City of Philadelphia', as
'sold by John Thornton in the Minories and
Andrew Sowle in Shoreditch, London,
1683', could well be recreated in blackwork.
*(Reproduced from A Book of Old Maps
Delineating American History, Dover
Publications, 1969, by kind permission of
the publishers)*

$(11\frac{1}{2}$ in $\times 17\frac{1}{4}$ in) and it is of interest that William Bradford, son-in-
law of one of the original London vendors of the map, Andrew
Sowle, established the first printing press in Philadelphia in 1685.

Details about this, and similar cartographical delights, are to be
found in Archibald Freeman's *A Book of Old Maps: Delineating
American History* (Dover Publications, 1969 edition of 1926
original). A keen blackwork embroiderer on the look-out for new
inspiration will find ideas and themes in many arts and reference
books not immediately of direct interest to the practical needlewoman.

Photographs of houses, and their embellishments, can also offer
ideas. A view (figure 76) of the main gates of the eighteenth-
century castle at Fertod in Hungary shows how effective a
wrought-iron pattern might be if worked in blackwork embroidery. Here the arabesque theme is brought to the forefront
once again.

International architectural themes recur throughout blackwork of
today. One popular device is that of the mosque. Perhaps the very
shaping of the domes and minarets associated with moslem
architecture are attractive to the geometric embroiderer: perhaps,

76 Arabesque inspiration from the wrought-iron gates at the eighteenth-century castle at Fertod, Hungary

alternatively, she is subconsciously reiterating the part that the Moors of many years ago played in the general heritage of monochrome decoration.

Gay B. Ayers of Farmington, Connecticut, worked her mosque (figure 77) on evenweave linen. Some of the architectural details are incredibly realistic: the main door of the mosque looks like the ornate carved wooden structure it would in fact be.

One form of architecture that is a 'natural' for blackwork transposition is the black-and-white timber-and-plaster construction found in many Tudor and mock-Tudor buildings in England.

Liberty's, the Regent Street store renowned around the world for its lawns, its other fine fabrics, its treasures from the east and elsewhere, celebrated its centenary in 1975. As part of the celebrations that included a major retrospective exhibition in the Victoria and Albert Museum and other important promotions, the store commissioned a special knitted sweater, designed by Clutch Cargo and made up with a main body length of 32.5 cm ($12\frac{3}{4}$ in). Part of the design, which shows the 'Tudor' facade of the store (figure 78), rebuilt in 1924, transposes beautifully (figure 79a, b) to counted thread blackwork embroidery.

77 Moorish inspiration and Moorish
architecture, a mosque by Gay B. Ayers,
worked on linen 59.7 cm × 33.6 cm (23½
in × 13¼ in). *(Gay B. Ayers)*

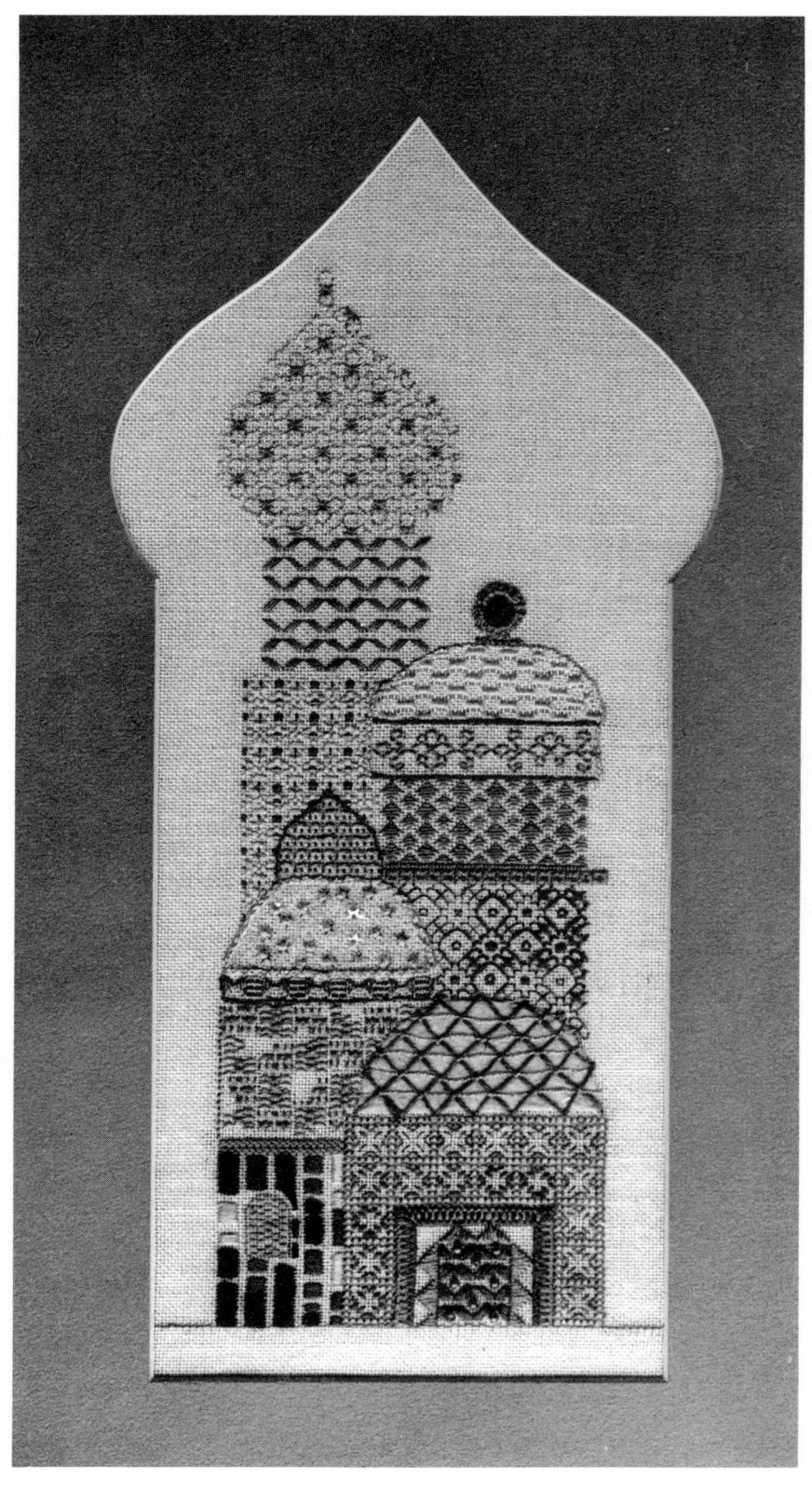

78 'Tudor' architecture, the black-and-white façade of the London Regent Street store of Liberty's, rebuilt in 1924

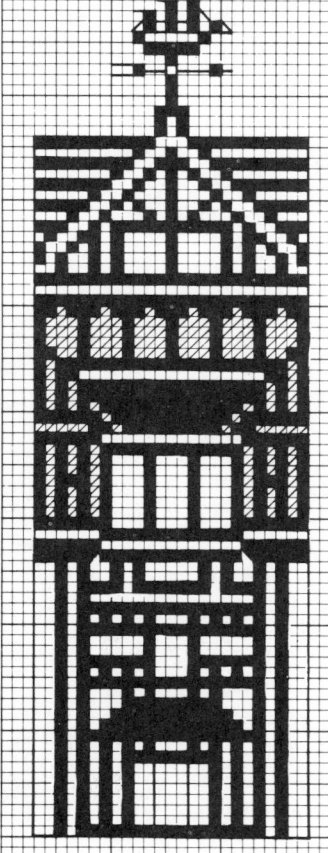

79 The façade was used as a design (figure 79a) for a special 1975 Liberty's centenniel sweater, 32.5 cm (12¾ in) long, designed by Clutch Cargo. The design can itself be transposed (figure 79b) to blackwork counted-thread embroidery

80 Landscape architecture—Wellington, New Zealand, with the Mount Victoria Look-out Station to the left horizon. The embroidery was worked by Cynthia Marks. *(Cynthia Marks)*

It has often been said that the architectural and geometric proportions of blackwork endear it not only to the embroiderer but also to the beholder: this is one reason why *blackwork* embroidery is more than usually popular with men. A view (figure 80) of Wellington, New Zealand, worked by Cynthia Marks shows the hills behind the city worked with filling stitches that give exact indication of the foliage in each spot: the hill to the left of her picture is worked in rice stitch to give a semblance of gorse and fir trees are worked in thorn stitch. Surmounting the horizon is the Mount Victoria look-out station with, not far away, the Admiral Byrd Memorial, shaped like an Antarctic explorer's tent in memory of Richard E. Byrd (1888–1957), the American naval pilot who discovered and charted so many hitherto unknown areas of the Antarctic.

Architecture is often conducive to reproduction in blackwork. Gillian Crowsen of Auckland took a 1972 newspaper advertisement for a Japanese cement producer as template for a blackwork embroidery (figure 81). The advertisement showed a horizon of skyscrapers and the textural effect of each building has been faithfully reproduced in the embroidery.

Photographs can offer alternative architectural inspiration. J. M. Bell, a member of Wellington Embroiderers' Guild, took her embroidery 'Wellington under Construction' from a photograph (figure 82). The partially built square block with crane on top is exactly worked (figure 82b) with geometric stitches, the beauty of the main chapel window is similarly recreated. But, of course, an embroiderer is allowed customary 'artist's licence' and J. M. Bell has therefore left out small noticeboards, lamp standards and other details—including traffic—not of consequence to her main design.

81 Advertising architecture—a Japanese newspaper advertisement recreated on a 22.2 cm × 26.7 cm (8¾ in × 10½ in) blackwork by Gillian Crowsen, of Auckland. *(Gillian Crowsen)*

One can learn much about architectural desgn from other parts of the world by looking at blackwork embroideries from the countries concerned. A trio of blackworked 'American houses' shows which house designs were popular in the past. Barbara Loftus, of Boulder, Colorado, worked a 'Charles Adams' sampler (figure 83), with twenty filling stitches used to give correct constructional feel. Virginia Hill Bornemann, of Hydesville, California, shows two popular local styles of building. 'Hydesville—Queen Anne/Victorian' (figure 84) gives a clear idea of a building wth bay windows, a patio and balconies. 'Hydesville—Victorian Farmhouse' (figure 85), illustrates the more compact architecture of the farmer's mansion with orchard and fertile land around.

82 Photographs and architecture (figure 82a) — a view of Wellington as interpreted by J. M. Bell on a 24.8 cm × 33 cm (9¾ in × 13 in) blackwork panel (figure 82b). *(J. M. Bell)*

83 American house—as portrayed by
Barbara Loftus in a panel 33 cm × 27.9 cm
(13 in × 11 in). *(Barbara Loftus)*

84 American house by Virginia Hill
Bornemann, 'Hydesville—Queen
Anne/Victorian', a panel 40.6 cm × 50.8 cm
(16 in × 20 in). *(Virginia Hill Bornemann)*

85 American farmhouse,
'Hydesville—Victorian Farmhouse' as
worked on a panel 43.1 cm × 63.5 cm (17
in × 25 in) by Virginia Hill Bornemann.
(Virginia Hill Bornemann)

Throughout the Middle East, women, their faces veiled from the sight of any men other than their husbands, hid themselves behind the mashrabiya (figure 86), a fretted screen, an eminently practical architectural feature that for centuries served as window, curtain, air conditioner and refrigerator. These wooden window screens first appeared in Egypt in the fourteenth century and some are still to be seen today in many countries in the Middle East. The fretted designs of a mashrabiya can often be ideally adapted to blackwork embroidery. The patterns are geometric or pictorial and occasionally they include inscription from the Koran. Mashrabiya designs (figure 87) offer, indeed, a wealth of interesting ideas for blackwork transposition since light—or chiaroscuro—plays so great a role in all blackwork. Fenestration is thus an obvious choice for much blackwork embroidery design. The stained-glass effect of two window panels (figure 88) embroidered by Stella Hales shows how effective blackwork windows can be. The inspiration for this embroidery came from a photograph in the colour supplement of a national newspaper.

Above and below . . . there are architectural themes all around. Floors of such diverse buildings as Hampton Court Chapel (figure 89) and a house (figure 90) belonging formerly to an early nineteenth-century gentleman, Mr Moses Morse, in London, New Hampshire, suggest patterns for basic blackwork transposition. Mr Morse's house was painted in 1824 and the interior included a bold checkerboard flooring painted originally in blue and buff squares (see *Country Life*, 3–10 January 1974, p. 33). The floor pattern show how striking the most simple of geometric forms, the alternating square, can be. And the miscellany is capped with designs (figure 91) taken from the vaulted ceilings of the fifteenth-century tower of Canterbury Cathedral, Kent, a building that traces its heritage to A.D. 597 when St Augustine arrived from Rome to baptize King Ethelbert of Kent and thus to pave the way for the conversion of all England to Christianity.

It is thus apparent that no designs are outside the scope of the blackwork enthusiast. And it follows naturally from the world of inspiration available that many blackwork embroiderers today are so enthusiastic in their approach and so technically skilled that they become prolific in their output.

What does one do with blackwork embroidery? And how should it be displayed? These are questions of vital importance to all embroiderers of today.

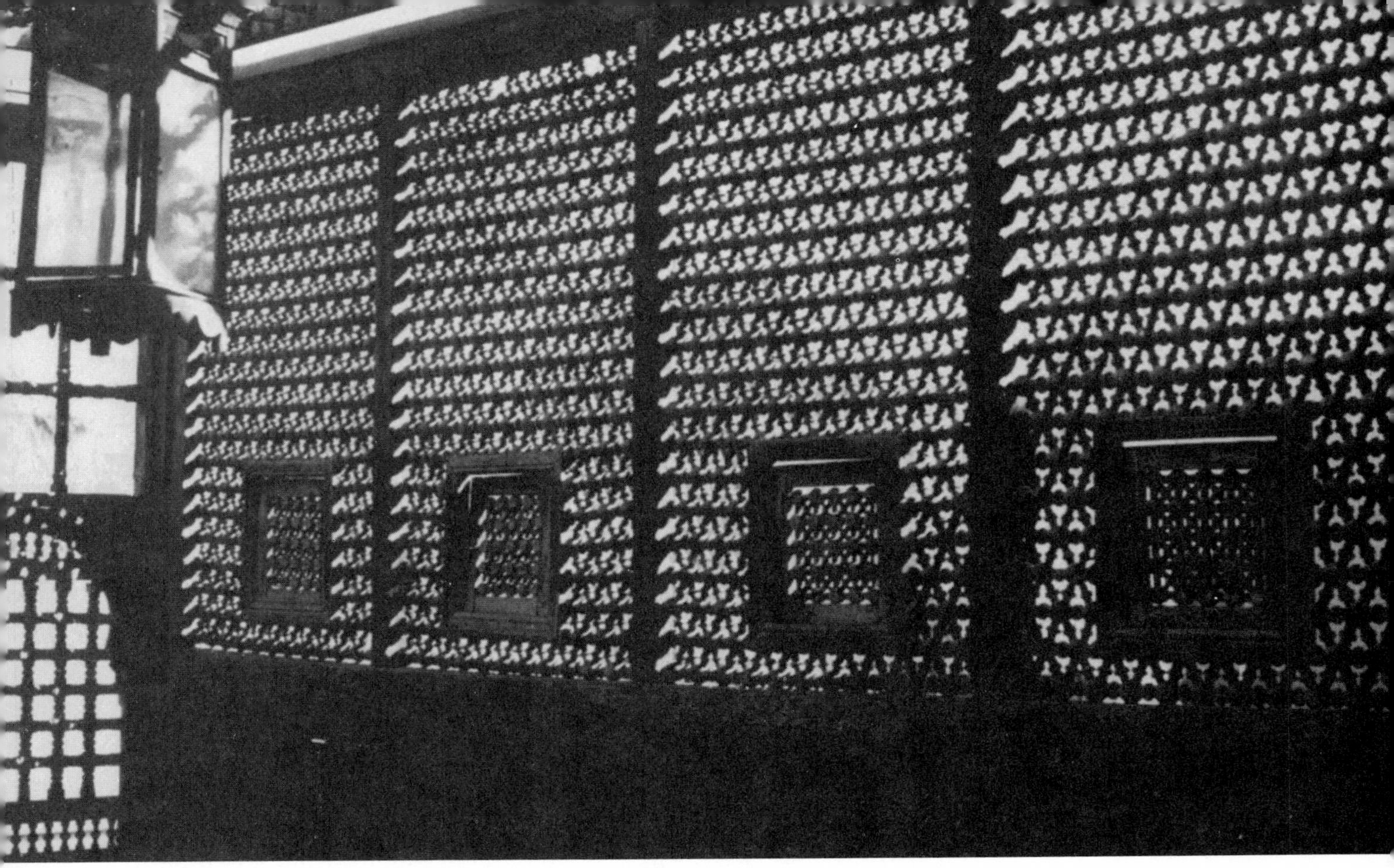

86 A mashrabiya, a fretted wooden screen through which discreet ladies of the Middle East could watch without being watched. *(Photograph by courtesy of* Aramco World Magazine*)*

87 Window designs, taken from a mashrabiya.

88 Window designs, copied from a
photograph of stained-glass windows in the
colour supplement of a national newspaper.
The embroidery 18.8 cm × 14.5 cm ($7\frac{1}{2}$
in × $5\frac{3}{4}$ in) was worked by Stella Hales.
(Stella Hales)

89 Floor designs, taken from the marble
design on the floor of Hampton Court
Chapel

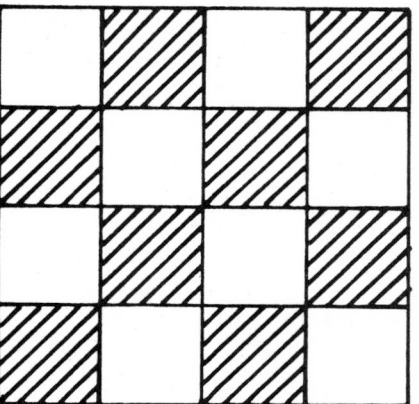

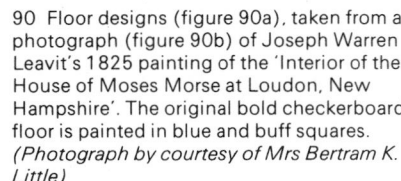

90 Floor designs (figure 90a), taken from a photograph (figure 90b) of Joseph Warren Leavit's 1825 painting of the 'Interior of the House of Moses Morse at Loudon, New Hampshire'. The original bold checkerboard floor is painted in blue and buff squares. *(Photograph by courtesy of Mrs Bertram K. Little)*

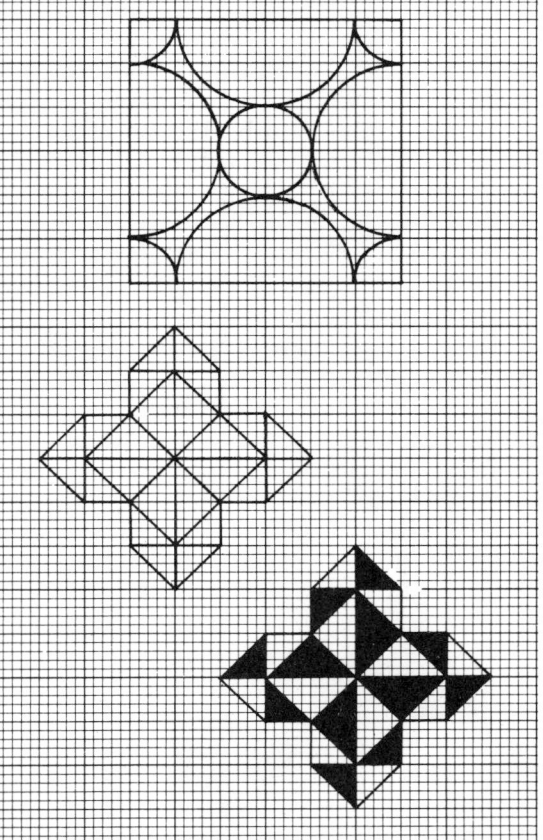

91 Geometric patterns taken from the vaulted ceilings of Canterbury Cathedral, Kent

8 Useful Blackwork

One of the most exciting of all embroidery exhibitions in recent years was that organized in Bloemfontein, in the Orange Free State, by Hetsie van Wyk.

Mrs van Wyk has been teaching embroidery since 1951. In 1975 she organized a 'one-studio show' in the National Museum. There was an entire section of blackwork embroidery and the pieces on show illustrated to how many uses this delicate form of needle-work can be put. The Bloemfontein Exhibition included table-cloths and napkins, tray-cloths, tea-cosies, bell pulls, banners and handbags. Blackwork is striking and it is therefore well suited, as a decorative art form, for the embellishment of so many items of everyday and special-day use.

The South African ladies can indeed be justly proud of the tablecloths they are today embroidering as heritage for tomorrow. Esther Geldenhuys, from Kroonstad, is co-author of a unique full-colour book on entertaining (*Cordially Yours*, 1973). Some of the most beautiful illustrations in this comprehensive book are those of a table set with a cloth that she embroidered, in blackwork, each roundel of the design constituting a new addition to her massive 'sampler' of stitches and geometric design.

Sometimes less mammoth cloths are nearly completely covered with different blackwork patterns. B. Cronje executed a geometric sampler (figure 92) in the form of a small cloth. She worked it to a design by Hetsie van Wyk; each of the van Wyk designs is an original and therefore when a needlewoman like Ria Wessels or one of her colleagues finishes a cloth into which she has put, literally, many years of work she knows that she has a unique piece of embroidery.

Two pieces of Ria Wessels' embroidery illustrate the dexterity and patience of her blackwork. A tea-cosy and a small circular mat (figure 93) are worked with a great variety of geometric patterns. Alternate diagonal cartouches of the tea-cosy design are bordered by corner mounts with arabesques at the inner angles.

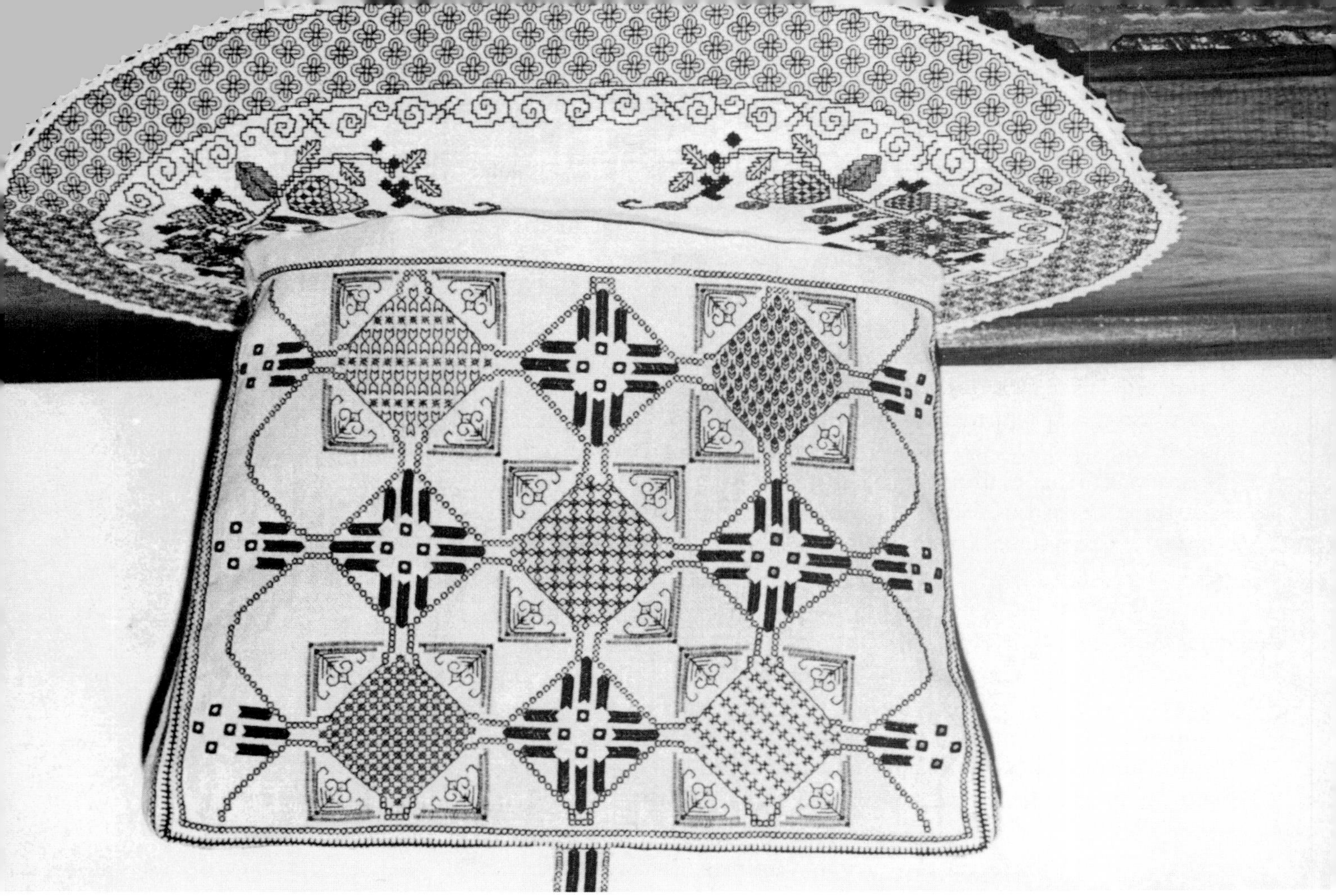

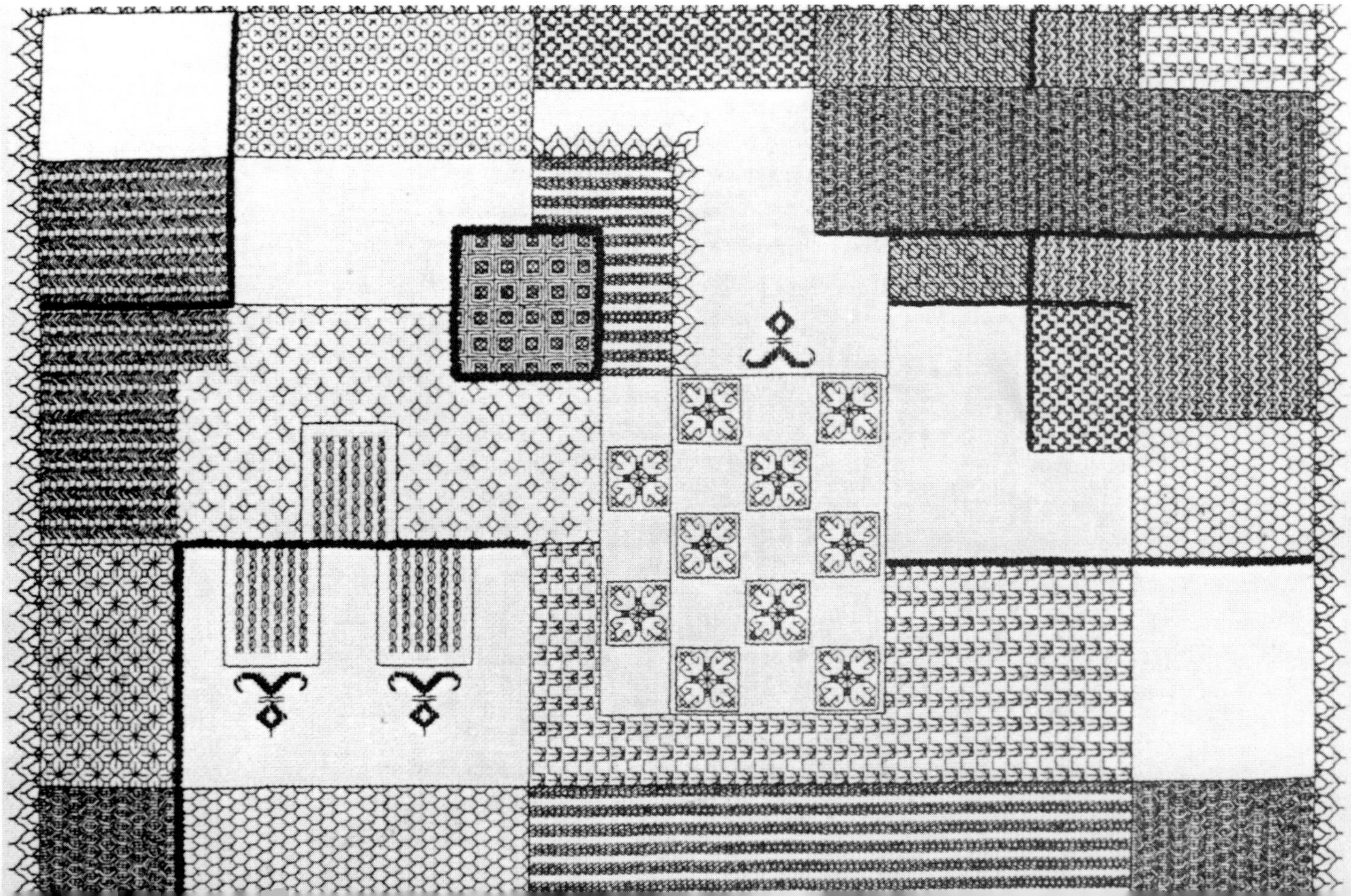

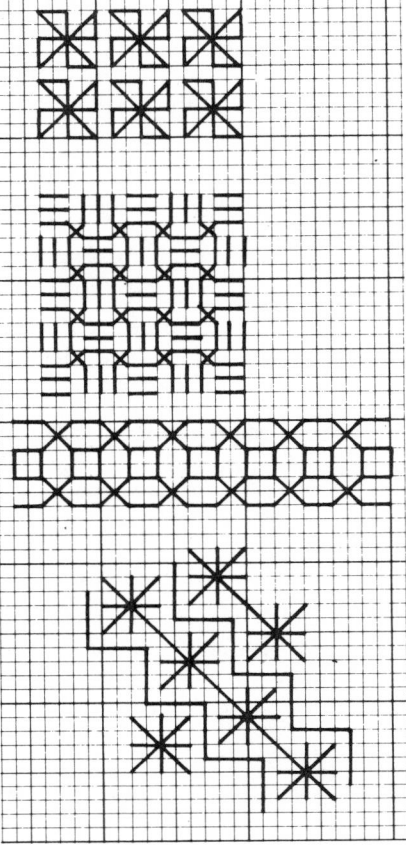

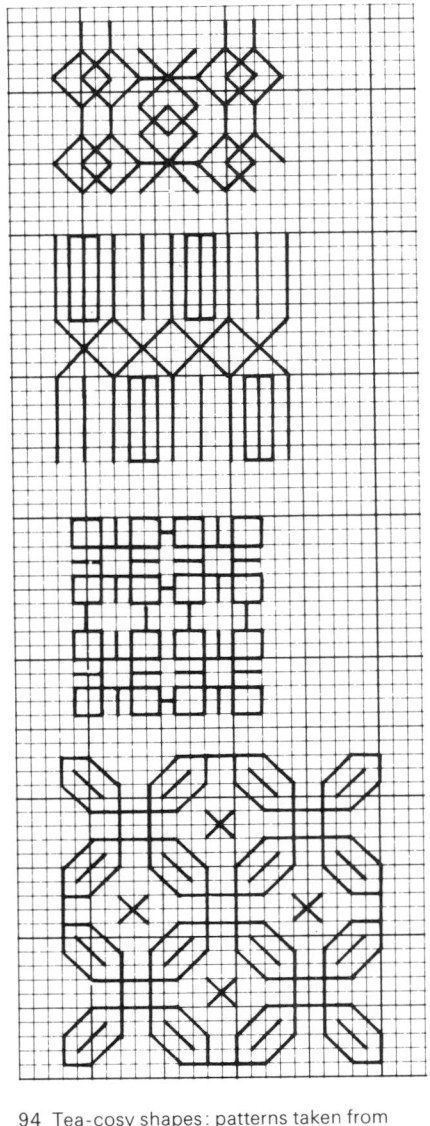

92 Blackwork cloth, 35.6 cm × 50.8 cm (14 in × 20 in), worked by Mrs B. Cronje to a design by Hetsie van Wyk. *(Mrs B. Cronje)*

93 Tea-cosy and cloth, designed by Hetsie van Wyk and embroidered by Ria Wessels. *(Ria Wessels)*

94 Tea-cosy shapes: patterns taken from the spout, handle, base and sides of a teacosy, 27.9 cm × 35.6 cm (11 in × 14 in) designed and executed by Karyn H. Katz. *(Karyn H. Katz)*

Although tea-cosies are not used so frequently in some countries of the world today, they do offer a useful and acceptable 'present form' for the blackwork embroiderer. Both facets of the cosy can be used for sampler embroidery. Karyn H. Katz, president of the Brooklyn Chapter of the Embroiderers' Guild of Amerca, worked her cosy (figure 94) with different patterns for the spout, the handle and the base of the design.

Because of the difficulty of aligning geometric blackwork to curvilinear shapes, embroiderers often prefer to work within the confines of a rectangular or square perimeter. It requires skill to place exactly a quartered design on a circular cloth. L. C. Farr of Palmerston North took the design for a round cloth (figure 95) from a larger tablecloth. Each quarter of the pattern constitutes a symmetrical design of a flower with foliage and hanging berries. The cloth is worked on Glenshee linen with thread count of 56 per 5 cm (28 per inch) and the design is worked in coton à broder, perle and fil à dentelles threads.

During the age of the first Elizabeth, ladies and their gentlemen wore assorted and beautiful pieces of costume blackwork. Today, as has been shown, the black-on-white 'shock' element of costume design is still provided by Madame Grès, the 'pop art' and 'op art' designers of the 'sixties and by other creators of haute couture and more accessible fashion.

Home-embroidered blackwork is not generally considered suitable as a decoration for today's fashion-conscious lady : it is frowned on even more for her avant-garde gentleman. But what is to stop an embroiderer producing a blackwork tie? It would be original, in both concept and design, and it might suitably complement the plain bright-coloured shirts and outerwear of today's man.

Shawls are back in high fashion. The regular costume and textile sales held by leading London auction houses are continuing to attract many buyers who bid for old clothes that they can actually *wear*. The blackwork shawl (figure 96) illustrated is a puzzle. It is embroidered with black silks on a soft white wool. The design is taken right through the ground fabric but, as the photograph shows, the pattern is much more dense on one side of the shawl. It was meant to be folded diagonally just to one side of the main half-way mark. At this stage the pattern 'transposes', with the heavier working on the *other* side of the wool. When folded over, therefore, the dense sides would be on one facet. The shawl is fringed along every edge. The design of the shawl is resplendent with buta (or kulka or kalka), the cone or palmette shape that has in the past been associated in the main with embroideries from the

95 Circular cloth designed by L. C. Farr. The
59.7 cm (23½ in) diameter cloth is a copy of
a larger tablecloth. *(L. C. Farr)*

96 Detail of a shawl, 1.75 m (68¾ in) square. *(University Museum of Archaeology and Ethnology, Cambridge)*

Indian subcontinent and from Iran. The repetition of double-headed cones around the outer borders looks as though of Middle East origin and, certainly, there is an Islamic air to the shawl. Its exact provenance is not recorded. The shawl is in a marvellous international ethnographic embroidery collection at the University Museum of Archaeology and Ethnology in Cambridge.

Since the shawl or scarf is today acceptable both as high fashion and as a practical accessory, blackwork embroiderers might be tempted to work their own. The personal aspect of such an embroidery is important. Embroidering something for oneself is incredibly satisfying—the feeling of achievement is akin to that of the gardener who grows tomatoes, courgettes or corn for the first time.

Handbags and evening purses offer similar scope for blackwork. Two small bags (figure 97) designed by Hetsie van Wyk, one embroidered by the artist and the other executed by Ansie Heyns, show how beautifully blackwork patterns can be mounted on the bag-frames available from most good needlework and similar stores. Finishing off such a 'miniature' blackwork project considerably adds to the final effect. Both these bags have a black silk tassel, both have side gussets and one has a long handle also stitched with blackwork designs.

Mounting and displaying blackwork are both important features of the overall effect of a finished piece. The alignment of a geometric embroidery demands the highest skills both in mounting and in display. Fortunately blackwork, unlike canvaswork and other forms of counted-thread embroidery, does not generally pull out of shape during working. It is not usually necessary therefore to subject a finished piece to 'blocking'. If a piece has become distorted during working, the embroiderer is recommended initially simply to pull the fabric back into shape, pinning it face downwards to a flat surface (perhaps to a piece of fibre-board covered with a clean towel or blotting paper) and gently to iron the embroidery—on the *wrong* side—with a steam iron. It is definitely not recommended at any time actually to dampen the blackwork.

Some of the most successful methods of mounting are the simplest. Virginia Hill Bornemann mounted her 'The Graham Grandchildren Family Tree' (figure 98) with all four edges turned back over a board. But because the pattern is exactly aligned—the bottom dips of the lowest line of zigzag stitching sit perfectly along the bottom of the picture—this easy method of mounting is, by its very lack of adornment, effective and very sophisticated. The embroidery is worked mainly in back stitch.

The same artist worked another blackwork as a banner (figure 99). Once again, a simple method of display becomes sophisticated because of its skilful execution. The design for the cock was taken from a Diner's Club advertisement and the banner was worked with coton à broder in back stitch, darning stitch and various filling stitches.

Many people prefer to have their blackwork embroideries professionally mounted. Glazing often detracts from the textural effect of embroidery but a simple frame, with no glass, can be an effective mount. A panel (figure 100) worked by L. M. Jones, a member of the Norfolk Branch of the Embroiderers' Guild, is mounted in a wooden frame with inner beading. Alternative methods of framing blackwork embroidery incorporate the use of suspension and

97 Two bags designed by Hetsie van Wyk. The one to the left was embroidered by the designer and the other was executed by Ansie Heyns. *(Hetsie van Wyk, Ansie Heyns)*

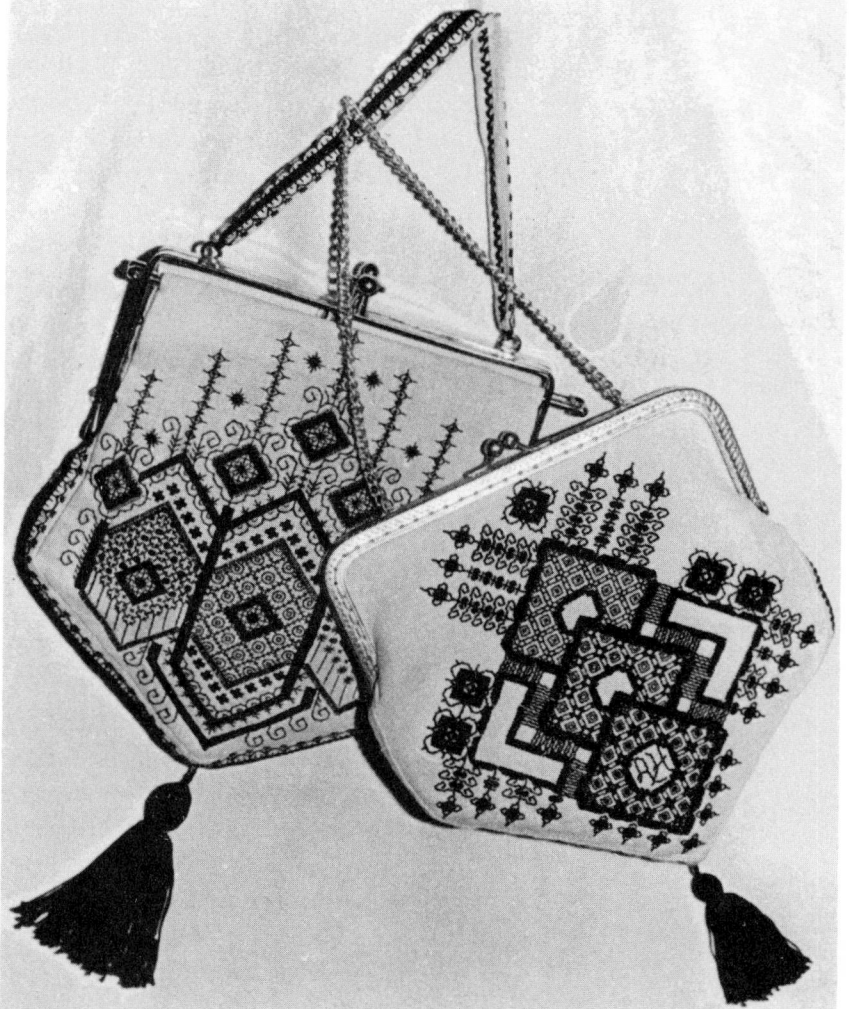

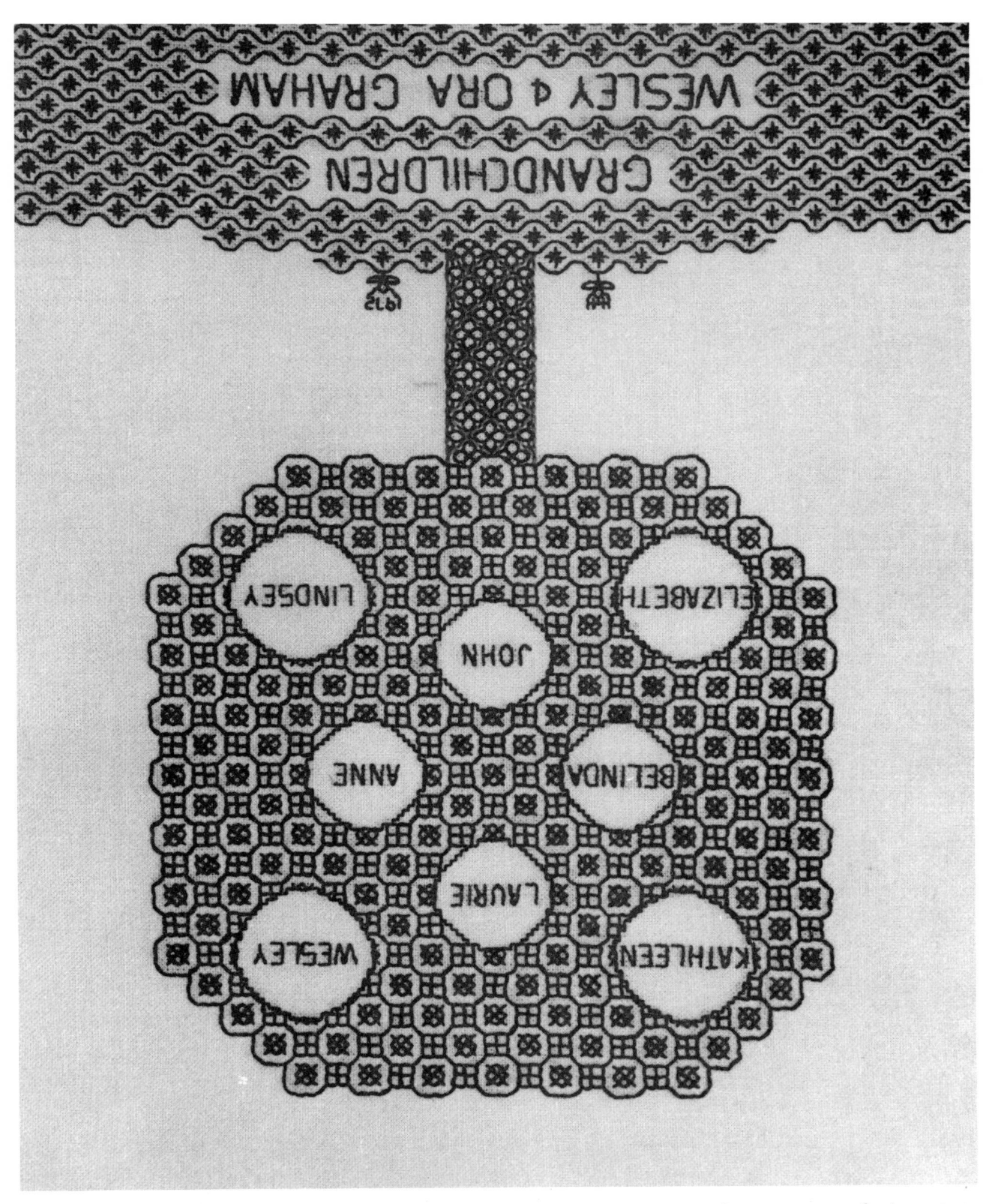

98 Mounting blackwork: a genealogical
embroidery, 'The Graham Grandchildren
Family Tree', mounted simply but exactly
over a backing board 57.1 cm × 43.2 cm
(22½ in × 17 in) by the artist, Virginia Hill
Bornemann. (*Virginia Hill Bornemann*)

99 Another method of mounting blackwork: a banner embroidery is suspended between two horizontal poles. The embroidery is 73.4 cm × 30.5 cm (29 in × 12 in)
(Virginia Hill Bornemann)

100 Traditional mounting for traditional work: a beautiful blackwork panel has been professionally framed and glazed. The embroidery is 33 cm × 45.7 cm (13 in × 18 in) and it was worked by L. M. Jones. *(L. M. Jones)*

101 Blackwork is fun! The embroiderer who worked this late sixteenth-century cloth, 106 cm × 88.9 cm (42 in × 35 in) overall, worked half the herringbone stitch from one side, half from the other. When the cloth is turned back, as it is in this photograph, the pattern is 'reversed'. *(Castlegate Museum of Textiles, Nottingham)*

102 The attraction of ethnographic design is shown in this trio of drawings: a, the design of a lady's wrap-around skirt, 60.9 cm × 5.26 m (24 in × 17 ft 3 in), from Zaire; b, the original 'hollow-tube' design could be worked in free-form blackwork in positive form; c, it could also be worked in reverse, negative, form. *(Original drawing reproduced by courtesy of the College Museum, Hampton Institute, Virginia)*

other do-it-yourself frames available today from good art suppliers.

As a corollary to the usefulness of blackwork, it is perhaps necessary here to introduce the exciting creative function of free-style blackwork.

Nearly all the pieces covered in a survey of blackwork through the ages must obviously exemplify the geometric element of the art. But even in some of the earliest known pieces of 'historical blackwork' an interesting individuality on the part of the embroiderer is noticeable. A coverlet (figure 101) in the collection of Castlegate Museum, Nottingham, is worked with a pattern of caterpillars in scroll surrounds. Half the design is worked in herringbone from one side of the cloth, the other half is worked, also in herringbone, from the reverse. This means that on one facet only the two lines of outer (reverse) stitches are shown and the 'heavy line' of the obverse therefore appears as a hollow tube on the reverse.

What imagination and creativity the late sixteenth-century or early seventeenth-century embroiderer had! It cannot be stressed too often what *fun* blackwork embroidery should be.

A hollow-tube pattern is found also on an early twentieth-century lady's skirt from Zaïre. The original wrap-around skirt was formed of a piece of cloth. The free-style design (figure 102a) could be transposed either to black tubing on a white ground (figure 102b) or to a reverse blackwork of white tubing on black (figure 102c).

Today many blackwork embroiderers are experimenting with the freedom of such 'free-style' work. Joan Forsyth worked her 'Doodle Design' (figure 103) in 'bluework', with various shades of blue thread on pale blue linen. The design was embellished with deep blue wooden beads and parts of the pattern were padded from behind to help the three-dimensional effect. Some segments were worked in single strands of cotton, others were embroidered in up to six strands of cotton. The main stitches used were double-knot stitch, chain stitch, running stitch and many pulled thread stitches. The idea was to obtain maximum shading and this was achieved partly by variation of thickness of thread, partly by balance of the area and partly by 'progressive working'.

New embroidery groups are continually being convened to promote the art in general and specific forms of embroidery in particular. The Practical Study Group is a group of teachers who want to share ideas and encourage creative embroidery. Daphne Nicholson's 'Sea Urchin' shell (figure 104) shows how free a

103 'Doodle Design' by Joan Forsyth, a
35.6 cm × 33 cm (14 in × 13 in) embroidery
worked in double-knot stitch, chain stitch,
running stitch and many pulled-thread
stitches. Beads were added and part of the
central surge of the design was slightly
padded from behind. *(Joan Forsyth)*

104 Daphne Nicholson's 'Sea Urchin', a
free-form blackwork embroidery, 12.7
cm × 12 cm (5 in × 4¾ in). *(Daphne
Nicholson)*

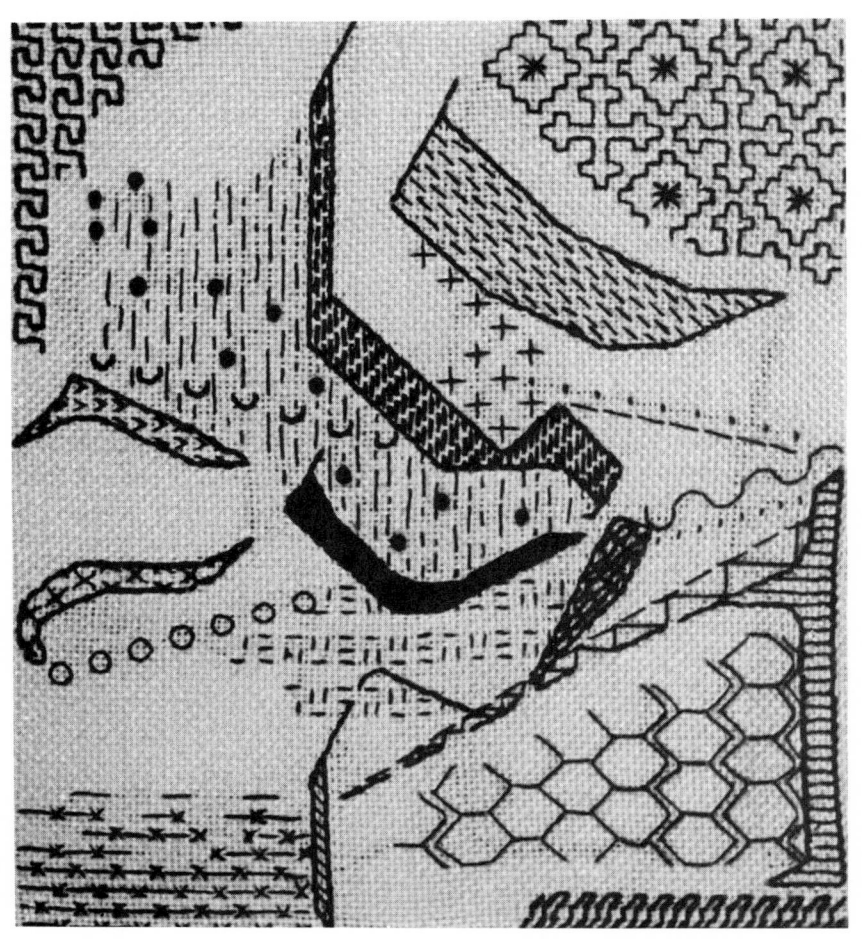

blackwork embroidery can become. It is a small panel and it has tremendous movement.

Blackwork has thus moved from the traditional to the creative aspect of design. It adapts to the time and to the place. Blackwork is a form of embroidery suitable for beginners and for those who are advanced specialists. It is an exciting and emphatic form of design.

Further reading

ALFORD, LADY MARIAN, *Needlework as Art*, Sampson Low, 1886. EP Publishing, 1975.

ANCHOR, *Modern Spanish Blackwork*.

CORNELIUS, ROSEMARY (with Peg Doffek and Sue Hardy), *Exploring Blackwork: The Sinbad Series No. 1*, Ellington, 1974.

DIGBY, GEORGE WINGFIELD, *Elizabethan Embroidery*, Faber, 1963.

DRYSDALE, ROSEMARY, *The Art of Blackwork Embroidery*, Mills and Boon, 1975.

THE EMBROIDERERS' GUILD, *Blackwork*, 1966.

* GEDDES, ELISABETH (with Moyra McNeill), *Blackwork Embroidery*, Mills and Boon, 1965.

GOSTELOW, MARY, *A World of Embroidery*, Mills and Boon, 1975. Scribner, 1975.

NEVINSON, JOHN L., *Catalogue of English Domestic Embroideries of the 16th and 17th Centuries*, HMSO, 1950.

NORDFORS, JILL K., *Needle Lace and Needle-Weaving*, Van Nostrand Reinhold Company, 1974.

PARKER, K. T., *The drawings of Hans Holbein in the Collection of His Majesty the King at Windsor Castle*, Phaidon, 1945.

RUSH, BEVERLY, *The Stitchery Idea Book*, 1974.

SCHUETTE, MARIE (with Sigrid Müller-Christensen), *The Art of Embroidery*, Thames and Hudson, 1964.

SYMONDS, MARY (with Louisa Preece), *Needlework through the Ages*, Hodder, 1928.

* THOMAS, MARY, *Mary Thomas's Embroidery Book*, Hodder and Stoughton, 1936.

WARDLE, PATRICIA, *Guide to English Embroidery*, HMSO, 1970.

WHITE, A. V., *Blackwork Embroidery of Today*, Mills and Boon, 1958.

WILSON, ERICA, *Erica Wilson's Embroidery Book*, Scribner, 1973.

*Reprinted by Dover Publications, Inc.

Index